2500 Jokes to Start 'Em Laughing

Robert Orben

Melvin Powers
Wilshire Book Company

12015 Sherman Road, No. Hollywood

Wilshire Book Company edition
is published by special arrangement
with Doubleday & Company, Inc., New York

Library of Congress Catalog Card Number 78-22538
Copyright © 1971, 1972, 1979 by Robert Orben
All Rights Reserved
Printed in the United States of America
First Edition

ISBN 0-87980-387-8

CONTENTS

Contents

Contents

Contents

INTRODUCTION

There is no better, faster, or more effective way to reach out and grab an audience's attention than by the adroit use of humor. An apt, well-timed joke can soothe the hostile, focus the uninterested, and hypo the enthusiastic.

Here are more than 2500 short, sharp laugh-getters that can be easily added to speeches, lectures, presentations, or casual conversation. They are arranged into several hundred categories for ease of selection. The subject matter is topical and the construction modern. Most are one-liners that develop the thought, the straight line, and the punch line in as few words as possible. The one-liner moves with a snap and a sizzle that create a sense of spontaneity lacking in anecdotes and stories. It is the humor of today.

Touching all speech bases, you will find openings and closings, plus random and specific comment invaluable to anyone who has ever been called upon to "say a few words." Even the material in the various subject categories has been arranged so that it forms a rough continuity. All you have to do is select and speak.

Those who can bring a smile, a giggle, or a belly laugh into our day are the most welcome of friends, neighbors, or business associates. It has often been said that humor is contagious. With the help of this book, you can be a carrier.

Bob Orben

ACCOUNTANTS

Our Accounting Department is the office that has the little red box on the wall with the sign saying: IN CASE OF EMERGENCY, BREAK GLASS. And inside are two tickets to Brazil.

Have you noticed how everybody's a comedian these days? Yesterday our accountant said he had a wonderful system for reducing our bills. I said, "That's great. What's it called?" He said, "Microfilm."

Our accountant has such a vivid way of putting things. Yesterday I asked him what our profit picture looked like. He said, "Well, let me put it this way: If you were a trapeze artist, you wouldn't want our net!"

We have a bookkeeper who's shy and retiring. He's shy $200,000. That's why he's retiring.

Some company reports use the Dolly Parton technique.
They put a good front on everything.

ACCOUNTS RECEIVABLE

Accounts receivable are bill-gotten gains.

Maybe you heard of our billing department.
It's known as the House of Ill Compute.

Life is so unfair. I have fourteen accounts that have gone bad and a secretary who won't.

There's nothing more frightening than sending a large shipment to a new account and then getting a D & B report that shows their assets are in the low five figures—$101.38.

I called up one account and said, "You know something? We've done more for you than your own mother." He said, "How do you figure that?" I said, "She only carried you for nine months. We've been doing it for a year!"

It's really a problem—especially around Christmastime. What do you give to the customer who has everything—and most of it's yours?

There's even the No-Pay Christmas Carol. When they start giving you those hokey excuses, you sing, "O come now, all ye faithless!"

When it comes to paying bills—he who hesitates is forced.

We use the Faye Dunaway Approach on collections.
Our bookkeeper's name is Faye, and if you don't pay in thirty days, she'll Dunaway!

Did you know they wrote a song about what our customers say when our bookkeeper calls them for money? LET ME STALL YOU, SWEETHEART.

Business wouldn't be so bad if customers didn't take a paper dispenser attitude toward their bills. When they find one in their letter box, they PULL DOWN AND TEAR UP!

I'm beginning to wonder if all our accounts are Russian. I think they read it: 30 days NYET!

ACUPUNCTURE

I suffer from a very expensive ailment—alcoholic acupuncture. I'm always getting stuck for drinks.

What's so unique about acupuncture? We've had people who practiced it for years. They're called muggers!

Let me make one thing perfectly clear—American doctors have always practiced acupuncture. The only difference is:
Chinese doctors give you the needle with the treatment.
American doctors give you the needle with the bill.

My doctor has taken up acupuncture but I don't think he's too good at it. Every time I drink a glass of water I look like a fireboat!

If you don't think acupuncture really works,
when was the last time you saw a sick porcupine?

As I understand it, acupuncture works on almost anything—with the possible exception of the Goodyear blimp.

Personally, I couldn't take acupuncture. I'm too squeamish. I need gas just to have my eyeglasses adjusted.

ADVERTISING

This happens to be SMALL BUSINESS WEEK.
If you want to keep your business small, it's easy.
Don't advertise.

Road signs are a real indication of what an area is like.
For instance, upstate you have signs saying DEER CROSSING.
In Yellowstone you have signs saying BEAR CROSSING.
In Africa you have signs saying ELEPHANT CROSSING.
And on Madison Avenue you have signs saying DOUBLE CROSSING.

They took a poll on Madison Avenue and here is what people in the
advertising industry are worried about most:
Inflation, unemployment, crime, and armpits. . . .
Not necessarily in that order.

Advertising has really changed our thinking.
This morning my wife put on eye shadow, eyeliner, and eyelashes.
I said, "What are you doing to your eyes?"
She said, "Making them look natural!"

You can always spot somebody in the advertising business. If he left
his troubles on the doorstep, you wouldn't be able to see the house.

I've been in advertising for twenty years now.
When I fill out a questionnaire and it says RACE—
I put down RAT!

Advertising has to be the most insecure business ever. I know one
agency that starts off every memo with: Now fear this!

There's a new deodorant called "Afternoon on Madison Avenue."
You put it on and you'll never be noticed. It smells of martini.

Every time they bring out a new product they call it IMPROVED.
Kinda makes you wonder what they were passing off on you last
month.

They always talk about beer as having full-bodied flavor. What does
that mean—full-bodied? You don't know whether to drink it or take
it to a motel.

If there were any truth in advertising, they'd call it fatteccine.

AGE

I know an eighty-year-old man who married a sixteen-year-old girl and the wedding invitations were so appropriate. His name was in Gothic type and her name was in crayon.

My grandfather is ninety-three years old and he still has a gleam in his eye. He keeps missing his mouth with the toothbrush.

I never believed in the tooth fairy until I lost one of my false teeth. And the very next morning I found something under my pillow—a plastic quarter.

You know you're old when they put all the ingredients for your birthday cake in a pan, light the candles, and it bakes itself!

You know you're over the hill when you stay in one of those hotel rooms with a mirror on the ceiling—and all you want to do is watch yourself gargle.

Sixty-five is when your sex drive goes into Park.

They say that fellas over sixty still have their sex drive—although sometimes it feels like they're taking it in an Edsel.

I'm at that age where I don't even breathe heavily at X-rated movies —unless they're one flight up.

You know you're slipping when you have to put tenderizer on puffed rice.

Old age is when the only thing you can really sink your teeth into is water.

No, Virginia, Polident is not a damaged parrot.

Kids say, "Never trust anyone over thirty." Senior citizens say, "Anything less than fifty-two and you ain't playing with a full deck!"

Old age is when parents find out that stockings support and children don't.

I'm at that cereal age. I'm beginning to feel my corns more than my oats!

I don't wanna complain about getting older, but do you know how it feels when a crook says, "Stick 'em up!"—and you have arthritis?

I don't even remember when I was young. Sometimes I think I went directly from Dr. Spock to Dr. Scholl's!

I'm beginning to think my wife lied to me about her age. Who do you know has a recipe for curds and whey?

Isn't it terrible the way people lie about their age? If my wife were as young as she says she is—the best man at our wedding would have been a cop!

It's amazing. My wife tells everybody she's twenty-nine and yet our wedding invitations went out with a three-cent stamp.

She was young when the ultimate weapon was a rock! . . .
When the Avon Lady was Mrs. Shakespeare.

AIR CONDITIONING

The nice part about air conditioning is, you finally know what to do with your winter clothes in July—wear them!

We had a big party for a returning serviceman last night. It was the air-conditioning serviceman. He brought back the part he went out for in August.

Did you ever pause in your daily activities and take a moment to think about deep, momentous, significant things? Like: What did hernia doctors do for patients before they invented portable air conditioners?

They say that a portable air conditioner really supplies you with cold air, and that's right. By the time you get three neighbors to help you carry it upstairs—it's November!

It's like I was trying to explain to my boss today—the only reason I keep a bottle in my desk is to ward off the chill from the air conditioning.

AIRLINES

I'm no flier. I even get dizzy looking into a plate of deep-dish apple pie!

I love it when they say, "Ladies and gentlemen, we are in a holding pattern over Kennedy Airport but we expect to land in just a few minutes." Then they start showing *Gone With the Wind*.

You can't imagine how they frisk you at airports these days. Embarrassing? I took off two hours before the plane did!

I think the airlines *should* have a special youth fare for Europe: $49 going and $3,488 return.

The airlines know what they're doing. They're building planes so big, pretty soon there won't be anybody left on the ground to complain about the noise.

I'm fascinated by these planes that carry three hundred people and have only twelve washrooms. Now I know what they mean by a holding pattern.

There's one problem with air travel. Over every airport in the United States today there are things that are stacked. These are called stewardesses.

But have you noticed how most stewardesses are a little deaf? They go up to a fella and say, "Is there anything I can do for you?" That's why I think they're a little deaf. They never hear his first request!

The airlines are having a terrible problem with seats—like finding enough people to fill theirs!

Airlines are so desperate for business, I called one of them and said, "What's the fare to Los Angeles?" The clerk said, "$150." I said, "That's too much." He said, "Let's talk."

It's scary. I flew on one plane that was so empty, the pilot and co-pilot were holding hands. I think that was the reason.

It's called the Terra Firma Airline. If its planes were firma, there'd be less terra!

I feel so sorry for airline pilots. I really do.
Do you realize when an airline pilot walks down the aisle to the washroom, he can never hurry?

AIR POLLUTION

Ashes to ashes; dust to dust;
If cigarettes don't get you, the atmosphere must!

They say the air is free. Sure it's free.
Look at it. Who'd want it?

Air pollution is really something. I never figured to see the day when indirect lighting is the sun.

It's amazing what air pollution is doing. For instance, we have flowers in our garden that are purple, brown, and yellow. What makes it so amazing, they're lilies!

Air pollution really upsets me. Somehow I never figured to see the day when artificial respiration would be better than the real thing.

Air pollution is so bad, I happen to know that leaves aren't falling—they're jumping.

I'll say one thing for this town: It's made me very polite. Today I tipped my hat three times. Once at a woman and twice to get the soot off.

Remember the good old days, when if you ate outdoors the black specks on your food were pepper?

We've got to do something about air pollution. I just saw the first robin of spring fall out of a tree.

The air in this city is unbelievable. Now I know why birds sleep on one foot. They're using the other to hold their nose!

A new organization to improve the environment sent Howard Cosell a button. It's for his lip.

A city agency said that air pollution is beginning to level off. That's right—at about the fortieth floor!

We could be in a lot of trouble. As I understand it, the city's going to deal with pollution as soon as it can see its way clear.

But air pollution has done wonders for raising kids. Yesterday I heard a mother say, "Junior, don't stick your tongue out at your sister. You'll get it dirty!"

AMBITION

I never asked for much out of life. I just wanted to be born into a family where soul food was beef Wellington.

Everybody is trying to get ahead of everybody else. It's like the whole world has turned into a subway seat.

Thomas Edison said that genius is 1 percent inspiration and 99 percent perspiration. I dunno. I hate to think of anyone that sweaty handling electricity.

They say that kids today don't know what hard work means. They certainly do. That's why so many of them are on welfare.

ANTIQUES

I go to one of those movie-rating antique shops. The proprietor looks G and what he does to you is X.

An antique is when you pay five hundred dollars for something the previous owner paid five dollars for—to cart away.

Antiques have become so popular, right now there are 15 million Americans who have things that are old, funny-looking, don't work, and are only kept around for sentimental purposes. Some of these are called antiques—and the rest are called husbands.

The whole technique in going into an antique shop is, when you see something you want, pay no attention to it. Spend all your time looking at something else, then just casually ask the price of the first item—and you'll really fool the proprietor. 'Cause up till then, he had been giving you credit for intelligence.

My wife is so crazy about antiques, I just realized what I'm married to—a junkie junkie!

My wife is kind of gullible. She has the only painting of the Lord's Supper that has a Diners Club card on the table

One time she spent three hundred dollars for a clock that belonged to the late King George III. I don't want to say anything about this clock, but now I know why he was late.

APARTMENTS

Apartment builders have finally come up with something to make a long story short—seven-foot ceilings.

Last night my wife shook me awake and said, "There's a robber in the house." I said, "I know. The landlord lives downstairs."

I'll tell you how much heat my landlord sends up. I have a bottle of pills that says: KEEP IN A COOL PLACE. I use the radiator.

When I took the apartment he said he sends up heat religiously. And he does—once a week.

We live in one of those high-rise apartment buildings. Very high-rise. This building is so high, the elevators show movies.

If you call the first floor, it's long distance.

We live in an apartment that's so high up, they give you three utilities—gas, electricity, and oxygen.

We live on the forty-ninth floor and we also have an apartment on the second floor—in case we want to spend the night in town.

Can you imagine living on the forty-ninth floor? We don't take out the garbage—we bring down the Commandments!

And it's really a problem living on the forty-ninth floor. Yesterday I called up the superintendent and I said, "You gotta do something. We're afraid to look down." He said, "Because of the height?" I said, "No. Because of the roaches!"

The rental agent said, "It comes with electricity, heat, and running."

I said, "Running what?" He said, "I dunno. We've never been able to catch one!"

And it's in a great neighborhood. When you leave the building, the doorman doesn't say, "Good evening." He says, "Good luck!"

ARMY

The Army saves you a fortune on newspapers. If there's trouble anywhere in the world, they send you right over. You don't have to read about it.

The Army thinks of everything. They gave me room and board, medical and dental care, a thirty-day vacation, travel, a $10,000 life insurance policy, and the chance to use it.

I went into the Army in 1945 when Selective Service wasn't being too selective. In fact, I had the only draft notice made out to OCCUPANT!

One fella even went down to the draft board wearing lipstick. The doctor said, "Do you always wear lipstick?" The guy said, "Always!" The doctor said, "Good. We'll send you to Alaska. You won't get chapped lips!"

I know a guy who put on lipstick, high heels, and carried a purse down to the draft board. It couldn't have worked out worse. The Army took him in and the doctor took him out!

In World War II we spent hours and hours doing all kinds of vital things in the defense of democracy—like policing the lawn. Remember policing the lawn? In those days we had lawns that were policed. Now we don't even have neighborhoods!

As I remember it, we had four deadly enemies—Japan, Germany, Italy, and cigarette butts. Not necessarily in that order.

I used to have nightmares about that lawn. One time I dreamed the Germans flew over and it was awful. They made a direct hit on that lawn. Not with bombs—candy wrappers!

When I went into the Army, we had 12 million men in uniform. It was terrible. It was so crowded, we were sleeping three to a bed. What made it so terrible, we were starting to enjoy it.

I once knew a general who claimed he lived like an ordinary enlisted man—but it's the first time I ever saw a pup tent with a wine cellar.

We used to have a saying when I was in the Army. If you have a difficult intellectual problem, always ask a sergeant. He'll know a private in his company who can solve it.

If I ever went back into the service, I'd like to fly one of those supersonic jets. It's not that I'm so crazy about flying. I'm just partial to anything that lets you retreat at 1,400 miles an hour!

Now everything is the New Army. The New Army is so permissive, sergeants no longer say, "Eyes right!" They say, "You's right!"

They're trying to run the Army like a business and it won't work. What if war is declared and two million G.I.s call in sick?

Experts say an all-volunteer Army will never work.
Oh, no? What about the Salvation?

ARMY CLOTHING

But I have to be fair. You know what I liked about the Army? They gave you your own clothes. When I was in the Army they had 12 million men and three sizes.

That's right. Three sizes: too big, too small, and out of stock.

But the Army really takes care of you. You can tell by the clothes you get. I think the whole idea of army clothes is to make the enemy overconfident! . . . I had a coat that was so long, it came with shoelaces! . . .

In those days, everything they gave you was olive-drab. Your shirt was olive-drab. Your pants were olive-drab. One day I fainted on the lawn and it took them three days to find me.

But I have to admit one thing. The shoes they gave us were absolutely waterproof. If it rained, not a drop leaked out!

The old Army did strange things. Every time they gave you a pair of shoes you had to smear something on them to make them waterproof. I heard "waterproof" and right away I got worried. I didn't know if I was sailing to Europe or walking!

I had one big problem in the Army. I could never stand the winter uniform. Particularly the pants. I know wool itches but this was like Brillo with cuffs.

ARMY FOOD

I know this sounds strange, but I used to love army food—especially the coffee. I used to drink three cups of this coffee, go down to the local burlesque show, and yell, "Put it on! Put it on!"

Army coffee is always having to say you're sorry.

The Army had a knack for putting the right man in the right job. They drafted a brain surgeon whose hand was so steady he could cut to one millionth of an inch—and the Army really used him. On Sunday, he was the one who cut the roast beef.

We used to have quaint expressions for army food like S.O.S.—Save Our Stomachs. Don't get ahead of me like that.

I spent three weeks in a hospital because of army food. Suffered from a very rare disease—terminal lamb chops!

We had the only outfit where if the sergeant found a bottle on you— it was bicarbonate!

You have no idea what the food was like in the Army. For punishment they gave you seconds!

You had a little hint that the food wouldn't be too good from the basic army place setting—knife, fork, spoon, and cardboard container.

ASTROLOGY

·"Dear Mr. [YOUR NAME]. I would like to cast your horoscope. Could you tell me what sign you were born under?" "Yes, I was born under the NO PARKING sign. Dad said he knew the way to the hospital and Mother believed him."

I can remember when if a woman wanted to have a baby, the first person she talked to was her husband. Now it's her astrologer.

My wife won't make a move until she checks with her horoscope. Like last night the lights were low, soft music was playing, we each had a glass of champagne. I gave her a nudge and she said, "No." I said, "What do you mean, no?" She said, "Venus is not in the ascendancy." I said, "It doesn't have to be. I am!"

My wife really believes these horoscopes. This morning she's reading one of them in bed—suddenly she gives me a terrific rap in the head. I said, "What are you doing?" She said, "That's for next week!"

Personally, I don't believe in astrology. I've only known one person whose life was influenced by the stars—and he was an agent.

ASTRONAUTS

If I were an astronaut, I'd be one of the backup pilots. The minute they tried to put me in a spaceship, would I back up!

I'm so chicken, you ain't never gonna see me on the moon until I can get there in something civilized—like an elevator!

I had a terrible nightmare last night. I dreamed our gardener planted a flag on the moon—and it died.

Isn't it amazing? We go all the way to the moon to pick up rocks— and here on Earth we don't even pick up beer bottles!

AUTUMN

Autumn is when Mother Nature goes through a change of leaf.

Autumn is when leaves slowly turn from green to brown to gold to litter.

My neighbor loves each autumn;
For him it works out fine.
My apples fall in his yard;
His leaves fall into mine!

I don't care how beautiful they are, I still say the only man who ever enjoyed falling leaves was Adam.

Do you realize that if Sir Isaac Newton hadn't opened his big mouth, leaves might be falling *up?*

Isn't it fantastic how the weather has changed? It's the first time I ever saw lawn mowers with snow tires.

I always get a little sad on the last day the beaches are open before they close for the winter. I suddenly realize my eyes are on their last legs.

Autumn is when every man in America gets dressed up and has that certain air about him—mothballs.

My wife puts mothballs in everything. I mean, I can understand mothballs for sweaters, mothballs for jackets, mothballs for suits—but in jockey shorts? . . . I put on a pair this morning and by the time I reached the living room I'd invented three new dance steps.

October is when you open your storage closet and find you have a religious wardrobe—Holey! Holey! Holey!

I'm getting a little worried about my winter clothes. Yesterday a moth flew out of our closet, tapped me on the shoulder, and said, "You should be so kind, which way is Weight Watchers?"

BABIES

We buy everything on time. We haven't even paid for the baby yet. As of last Tuesday we owned two legs and a navel!

It now costs $750 to deliver a baby. This may not seem like much to you but it could ruin a salmon!

I'm really shook up. Last week we had sixty-two dollars' worth of food go bad. The baby-sitter had lockjaw.

BACHELORS

It isn't easy being a single fella these days. I've got a mother who wants me to eat and a doctor who wants me to diet.

I try to ration myself. I only think about girls on days that begin with the letter *T*. Today, Tomorrow, Thursday, Thighday, Thaturday, and Thunday.

If you're forty-two and you're going out with an eighteen-year-old girl, you ask yourself some interesting questions. Like: "What wine goes with peanut butter?"

It's unnerving going out with beautiful but dumb girls. I took one to a concert by Yehudi Menuhin and she leaned over and whispered, "What's he playing?" I said, "The Beethoven Concerto in D Major, Opus 61." She just stared at me. I said, "A violin."

BALDNESS

I agree with that shampoo commercial on television. Split hair is a real problem. [SMOOTH BACK YOUR HEAD.]
Mine split about ten years ago.

I don't know why people call me bald. Just because everybody else has a narrow part!

You don't seem to understand. I am not bald. I just happen to have a Life Saver haircut. There's a hole in the middle.

BANK ROBBERS

I happen to be a very good character analyst. Just yesterday I was standing in a bank and a fella came in with a stocking over his head.

Well, just like that I knew he was one of two things—a crook or a very sloppy dresser.

Bank robbers are so relaxed these days. One fella walked into a bank wearing a mask—ran right into a cop. The crook pointed at his mask and said, "Good morning, Officer. I'm on my way to a masquerade ball." No answer. "I'm studying to be a surgeon?" The cop kept looking at the mask. The crook said, "Would you believe the world's worst case of acne?"

Yesterday a crook held up a bank and told the teller to put $10,000 into a brown paper bag. Well, we can put a stop to that. All we have to do is register brown paper bags.

Have you ever noticed how a bank robber who steals $5,000 gets ten years in jail—and a bank owner who milks it of $5,000,000 gets a suspended sentence? That must be some of that stainless steal you keep hearing about.

BANKRUPTCY

The saddest story I ever heard was about a businessman who was on the brink of bankruptcy. Seeking solace, he turned to his copy of the Good Book, opened it at random, and the first thing he saw was Chapter Eleven.

The nice part about selling to a firm that goes bankrupt is, you get the business before, during, and after.

My former business had nothing to do with football but it did wind up in the hands of a receiver.

BANKS

Banks have a very interesting philosophy. You give them your money to keep—and if you try to borrow it back, they want to know if you're good for it!

My bank is getting a little sneaky. They gave ballpoint pens to all their depositors. Now they're printing the withdrawal slips on wax paper!

What this country really needs is a bank where you can deposit a toaster and they give you $5,000!

I go to the bank a lot. Last week I got $5,000 as a home improvement loan. I'm sending the kids to college.

I never knew why banks called them "personal loans" until I took one out. I missed three payments and did they get personal!

Isn't that nice? My bank just gave me one of those scenic checkbooks. It has pictures of rolling prairies, soaring mountains, majestic forests, stately rivers, and towering cities. It's like my account—overdrawn.

Even my bank doesn't have confidence in me. I have the only checks in town with three things printed on them—my name, address, and "INSUFFICIENT FUNDS."

Be careful of those calendars the banks give you to help you keep track of your payments. I saw one with sixteen months on it.

Everything is relative. To a banker, prurient interest is 18 percent.

BANQUETS

BEFORE A HUGE BANQUET: Tonight I want you all to forget your problems, relax, and enjoy yourself. After all, isn't it ridiculous how little it takes to upset people? Right now I could say two words that would ruin the evening for every waiter in this room. What are the two words? Separate checks!

INVITATION TO A CONVENTION BANQUET: Dinner will be served at seven as the orchestra plays "It's Delicious, It's Delightful, It's Deductible!"

OPENING FOR A BANQUET: It's a pleasure to see you all here tonight— the big shots, the little shots, and those who have just come in from the cocktail hour—the half-shot!

BASEBALL

Spring is the time of year when you can always tell a real baseball fan. He has the TV set overhauled, orders six hundred cans of beer, forty pounds of potato chips, three hundred TV dinners, and leaves a call for October.

I really don't know much about baseball. To me, an exhibition game is nine fellas coming out wearing raincoats.

I go out to the ball park maybe two or three dozen times a year. I'm not too thrilled with baseball but I'm crazy about undercooked hot dogs!

Between peanuts, popcorn, Cracker Jacks, and hot dogs, what the seventh inning stretches is you!

I gotta tell you. Yesterday I got a phone call from my Aunt Sophie. She was in a police station. I said, "What happened?" She said, "I'll tell you what happened! I was at Shea Stadium, something dropped into the field seats, and they wouldn't let me keep it!" I said, "A baseball?" She said, "A catcher!"

October is when 50 million marriages are threatened by the eternal triangle—a wife, a husband, and the World Series.

If you're a baseball fan, October is when you discover your wife left you in May.

My wife doesn't like baseball. She can never understand why a pitcher who gets $100,000 a year needs relief.

I know a left fielder who's very upset. He was sold for $80,000—by his wife.

I was watching a game yesterday.
The pitcher was warming up in the bullpen. I know he was warming up—he was reading *Playboy*.

As the nude ballplayer said to the coach, "Center fielder? I thought you said centerfolder!"

[NAME OF BASEBALL PLAYER IN THE DOGHOUSE] is doing such a fantastic job, yesterday the fans got together and gave him something—a ten-yard head start.

I'll say one thing for the [LOSING TEAM]. I didn't think anything could be in the cellar this long and not be an oil heater.

I feel a little sorry for the [LOSING TEAM]. They finished so far back, they came in fourth in another League—the Little.

You know who should have the world's greatest baseball team? Mexico! You drink the water down there and you better reach home!

A real fan is someone who thinks there's something wrong with his TV set—because every time he turns it on, the [CELLAR TEAM] lose.

The San Diego Padres are enough to make you give up one or the other—baseball or religion.

I don't know what's happening to this world.
I just saw a bubble gum card that folds out.

I was walking downtown when a girl stopped me who must have been a major league umpire. She kept saying, "Play? Ball?"

BASKETBALL

My daughter isn't very athletic, so you can understand why I'm a little upset about her last letter. She said she made the basketball team.

If you have to go in for a sport, forget golf—take up basketball. You don't get wet on rainy days; there's no walking; and the holes are the right size!

A basketball coach just came up with a terrific idea to get eight-foot players—seven-foot girls!

Everything is relative. To Toulouse-Lautrec, Napoleon was a basketball player!

BATHING SUITS

You know what bothers me at the beach? Those girls who lie face down in the sand and then unhook the top of their bathing suits. It's enough to give you the peeps!

Have you seen the latest? There's a nude-look bathing suit that's so realistic, it comes with stretch marks.

I won't say what bathing suits like this do to a normal, red-blooded American boy—but I was looking at one when a terrible thing happened. Somebody stepped on my tongue!

Did you hear about the girl who was a sensation at the beach? All she wore was a wrap—Saran!

I said to her, "There's something about that bathing suit I really like." She said, "It's nothing." I said, "That's it!"

BEACH

I'll tell you one thing. Anyone who says this country is in bad shape hasn't been to the beach lately.

It's one of those Bill Bailey beaches. You take one look at what the girls are wearing and you don't want to go home!

They say you should never go swimming right after a heavy meal and I never knew why. So one day I tried it and now I know why. You take four strokes, burp once, and you're right back where you started.

I like to watch the way people go into the ocean for the first time. Especially the ones who take five steps into the water and then go like this: [DUNK QUICKLY, BENDING YOUR KNEES SO THAT YOUR BODY DIPS DOWN AND THEN BACK AGAIN]. I've heard of testing water with your elbow, but this is ridiculous!

BEAUTY CONTESTS

This is the time of the year when they hold all those big beauty contests. You know what a beauty contest is. That's where ten gorgeous girls are in bathing suits—and five middle-aged judges are in heaven!

There's only one drawback for a fella my age in being a beauty contest judge. There's no money but you do get your meals. All day long you eat your heart out!

I went up to the fella running the beauty contest and I said, "Are you the head judge?" He said, "Yes. I'm the head judge!" I said, "Good. I'll take the legs!"

If you ask me, there's only one thing better than being a judge in a beauty contest. Being the tape measure!

It's fascinating talking to the contestants. The first girl said, "I'm a perfect 36 and tip the scales at 110." The second girl said, "I'm a perfect 38 and tip the scales at 115." The third girl said, "I'm a perfect 44—and the scales don't tip. I do!"

You should have seen this girl. I've never seen skin so well organized in all my life!

BEN HUR

We watched *Ben Hur* on television, and wasn't that a great chariot race? Charlton Heston cut off the driver on his right; sideswiped the one on his left; rammed the one up ahead. Then came that wonderful scene where they canceled his insurance!

And during most of the picture, Charlton Heston was wearing this Roman miniskirt. It was fascinating. Now I know why they called him Ben Hur.

Ben Hur is the story of the early Christians. Today we still have early Christians. They're the ones who get to sit in the back of the church.

BIBLE

If God had believed in permissiveness, He would have given us the Ten Suggestions.

As Moses said to the multitude when he showed them the Ten Commandments, "You might say they're nonnegotiable demands."

Two priests of the Golden Calf are listening to Moses tell the multitude about the Ten Commandments. Finally, one leans over to the other and says, "Eight years of grammar school, four years of high school, four years of college, four years of seminary, here we are on our first gig, and who comes along—Big Mouth!"

The multitude was very upset over getting the Ten Commandments, and so was God. He had dictated fifteen!

Youth has turned to religion. You can tell.
Last week I was mugged for my Bible.

The latest thing is musical versions of the Bible.
It's incredible. One of them has Matthew, Mark, Luke, and John singing: "If They Asked Me, I Could Write a Book."

Sometimes I wonder if the Bible is good for business. Like if the meek do inherit the earth, who's going to collect the bills?

BIRTH CONTROL

When it comes to birth control, you just can't beat a good fight!

If you're living with your wife's parents, the best birth control device is a bed that squeaks!

They now have a foolproof method of birth control. If you and your wife want to start a family, you call them up, and they send over a teenager.

My name is [FIRST NAME] O. [LAST NAME]. I was an unplanned addition to our family. The O stands for "Ooops."

My mother had eight kids. To her, birth control was making it to the delivery room.

Now here's the plan: We combine Raid and the Pill.
It's for people who want to get the bugs out of their sex life.

They just came up with a legal definition of the Pill.
It's an accessory-before-the-sack!

Shakespeare was so far ahead of his time, he even wrote a play about the Pill. It's called *Love's Labour's Lost*.

A modern girl is someone who takes vitamin pills to put her in shape and birth control pills to keep her that way.

Girls, you just can't win. If you take the Pill, you get side effects. And if you don't take the Pill, you get front effects.

Birth control will never work. Somehow I just can't see proud grandparents showing off pictures of the Pill.

According to the Census Bureau, the birth rate has dropped dramatically. I don't know what's happening to this country. We have movies that are rated X and bedrooms that are rated G.

England also has a declining birth rate but over there it's a different problem. Have you ever heard "The Anniversary Song" in England? "Oh, how we danced on the night we were wed; we never made love 'cause we're much too well bred!"

BIRTHDAY PARTIES

When it comes to birthday parties, mothers fall into two groups. Those who think a birthday party for twenty-four five-year-old kids can be organized, educational, and fun—and those who have had one!

You can always tell the experienced parents at a children's birthday party. They don't give the kids napkins—drop cloths!

Yesterday my wife held a birthday party for two dozen five-year-olds. I asked her how it went. She said, "Don't ever let me forget the Pill."

A kid's birthday party is very educational. One of the first things you learn is never to serve five gallons of lemonade in a house with two bathrooms.

It was like a traffic jam. You've never seen so many people stop and go!

And it's just amazing the names mothers teach their kids for this. One little kid came running up and said, "I have to wee-wee!" I said, "Wee-wee?" A second kid said, "I have to tinkle." A third kid said, "I have to number-one." A fourth kid said, "I have to sissie." A fifth kid said, "I have to go to the bathroom." I said to the first kid, "Is that what you have to do—go to the bathroom?" He said, "No more."

Thanks to mothers, Berlitz has a brand-new language:
Spanish, French, German, and Potty!

BIRTHDAYS

It's amazing how many Sweet Sixteen parties are canceled because of sickness—morning sickness.

I don't want to start any trouble, but have you noticed how a lot of people celebrate their birthdays television style? They celebrate their thirty-fifth birthday, and every year after that is a rerun!

Birthday presents can be expensive. One time we gave our daughter a doll that drinks and wets. Cost us ten dollars for the doll and forty-five dollars to retrain the dog.

I bought my son a bicycle for his birthday and I hid it where he'll never find it—his bathtub.

My boss has a peculiar sense of humor. For my birthday he gave me an antique bed warmer—a seventy-year-old call girl.

BODY-BUILDING

You know those body-building schools? My agent submitted me to one and the next day he called me up. He said, "I have good news and I have bad news. The good news is, they want you to pose for before and after pictures with Don Knotts." I said, "That's great. What's the bad news?" He said, "You're the before."

I have the kind of figure that looks great in tapered shirts. Particularly if I wear them upside down.

I don't want to complain about my body, but I didn't know God made Edsels.

Every morning I get up, bend over, and touch my toes.
Unfortunately it's with my stomach!

Every day my wife bends over and touches the floor fifty times. It's not exercise. It's picking up the kids' clothes.

The only thing my kids have ever picked up is chicken pox.

If you want to keep fit, there are two ways to touch your toes. Either you go down to them—or get careless with a power mower and they'll come up to you!

You know what's a great exercise? Weight lifting!
Well, it's not really the weight lifting. It's the running around you do when you drop one on your foot.

Weight lifting has made stars out of a lot of people—Mr. America, Mr. Universe, Dolly Parton.

BOOKS

Have you read some of the books they're selling these days? I saw one book that was so daring, the last page was a summons!

It's the kind of book that convinces you the pen is mightier than the sword. The pig pen, that is.

I can always tell when I'm going to give birth to an idea. My writer's cramps start coming two minutes apart.

I love to read. I once went through every page of the Encyclopaedia Britannica and it really taught me something: Never hide a five-dollar bill without marking the place!

The first thing you have to overcome when reading a children's book to your five-year-old—is nausea.

Have you seen any of these children's books? They're all about Jane, Dick, and Spot. Spot is a dog—and Jane is nothing to brag about either.

But you do get involved in these stories. I read one—JANE LIKES BREAD. JANE LIKES OATMEAL. JANE LIKES ICE CREAM. JANE LIKES PICKLES. You don't think . . . ? Naaaahhhh!

BOSS

Please don't think of me as the boss. Think of me as a navigator on the Sea of Confusion.

You remember the boss. He's the crank that gets the wheels of progress started.

You can understand why some employees have a hard time by analyzing the word BOSS. That's a backward double S.O.B.

A boss is like the center on a football team. He always feels things are going on behind his back.

For a real quick energy boost, nothing beats having the boss walk in.

A real boss is someone who puts a sign reading SUGGESTION BOX—on the paper shredder.

Nowadays you can always tell a boss with compassion. He doesn't let you go. He just says you've been de-hired.

I didn't say the boss is quick to fire. I just said they're now calling his office Boot Hill.

I don't want to say anything about my boss, but you know how some people worry about being replaced by a computer? I worry about being replaced by a slave.

Maybe you know my boss. He's the one who expects a maximum effort for a minimum wage.

You remember the boss. He's the one who believes that work is the only way to repair a coffee break.

I won't say the boss is a slave driver but he just posted a sign saying: "NO PARKING 9:00 A.M. to 5:00 P.M." What he posted it on was my chair.

I'll say one thing for the boss: He's fair.
Yesterday he came up to me and said, "[YOUR NAME], I'd like to give you the day off—but if I did, I'd have to do the same for everyone else whose wife gave birth to quintuplets on her fiftieth birthday."

My boss thinks I'm a white-collar worker.
My laundryman would give him an argument!

Bosses who hire relatives have a payroll that just won't quit!

It's easy to tell the people in our office who get along with the boss.
They're the ones with shoe polish on their lips.

Somebody must be asking the boss for a raise.
I'd know that laugh anywhere.

I asked the boss if I could get a raise and he said, "Because of the fluctuational predisposition of your position's productive capacity as juxtaposed to the industry standards, it would be monetarily injudicious to advocate an increment." I said, "I don't get it." He said, "That's right."

I knew the boss was going to talk about my salary when he said it's the little things that count.

Now I know why they call it take-home pay.
You wouldn't want to be seen with it in public.

My boss is all heart. He really is. He's the one who tried to buy the lifebelt concession on the *Titanic.*

I told my wife the boss saw me today and said, "There's a man on his way up!" She said, "That's great. What were you doing?" I said, "Buying elevator shoes!"

It's all in the way you look at it. Telling the boss what you really think of him can be called honesty, integrity, and self-assertiveness. It can also be called a do-it-yourself recession.

The boss just told us we're going to have a fire sale.
Anyone who doesn't make a sale is going to get fired!

BUMPER STICKERS

I bought a bumper sticker for my subcompact saying: HELP SAVE THE REDWOODS OF CALIFORNIA, OREGON, AND WASHINGTON. It wrapped around twice.

Do you think this could start a trend? I saw a bumper sticker saying: CODDLE EGGS, NOT CHILDREN!

EATING DRIED BEEF IS JERKY.

AESOP IS ALIVE AND A GOVERNMENT SPOKESMAN.

USHERS ARE COMPULSIVE SEATERS!

LAKE ERIE REALLY IS.

BIRDWATCHERS ARE CHEEP DATES.

FOG IS AN EXTREMIST.

A.A. MEMBERS MAKE SOUSE CALLS.

JACK THE RIPPER IS ALIVE AND WELL AND PROCESSING PARCEL POST.

MAGICIANS ARE A VANISHING SPECIES.

SEN SEN HIDES A MULTITUDE OF GINS.

WELFARE ROLLS COULD USE SOME SHORTENING.

MEXICAN FOOD IS A PEPPER TIGER!

INTUITION IS A CASE OF MIND OVER DATA.

RACIAL PREJUDICE IS A PIGMENT OF YOUR IMAGINATION.

SUMMER STOCK IS A USED STAR LOT.

CONSERVATISM IS A STEP IN THE RIGHT DIRECTION.

WATER SKIERS ARE A DRAG.

BUSINESS

Getting ahead in business is like owning a twelve-year-old car—the most important thing is push!

I'm so busy, the only breather I've had was an anonymous phone caller.

In business, an ounce of future is worth a pound of past.

Work is important. If it wasn't for work, where would people rest up from vacations?

A partnership is when you hope to get, together.

Frankly, I'm doing very well in business. I have the Murine concession at the [LOCALIZE] Bus Terminal.

Business is really looking up. We carpeted our bathroom this year, and if we do as well next year, we're going to carpet the path out to it!

Our corner bakery is very successful because it operates on sound business principles—big profits, small turnovers.

Running a business these days is like Mickey Rooney dancing with Raquel Welch. The overhead is fantastic!

The trouble with most businessmen is, they don't use enough imagination. Like I have an idea that could double the business of any department store in the country. Make all the escalators UP.

The whole trick to being successful in business is to continually find new markets for your present product. For instance, has anyone ever tried to convince an octopus he needs underarm deodorant?

The free-enterprise system is always coming up with new ways to make money. For instance, there's a new type of barroom. It has free beer and pay washrooms!

I bought myself a franchise,
And maybe I'm just daft;
But what they call a gold mine,
To me is just a shaft!

I'm getting a little worried about the rat race.
I don't know if I'm slowing up or they're bringing in faster rats!

I made two big mistakes last year. The first big mistake was starting a new business. The second was starting it in a fireproof building.

We should have shown a bigger profit this year except that we did a lot that could be classified as R & D—Real Dumb!

I don't mind telling you, I've made a lot of mistakes in business. I once bought a parking lot that only had room for one car. What made it even worse—I drove to work!

I really don't have too good a business sense. Like, one time I bought the bar concession for A.A. meetings.

A rather disturbing thing happened last week.
A management team came into the office and gave everybody an aptitude test to see what they were best suited for. Most were best suited for unemployment.

Maybe things were better in the days before technology took over. Cigarette lighters didn't work but people did.

I wouldn't say I've been the greatest success in the world. In fact, when they want to teach someone the business from the ground up, they start with my job.

An employee is someone who welcomes suggestions with an open mind—and closed fists.

Yesterday I came home from a business dinner carrying a doggie bag and my wife met me at the door with three little words, "Woof! Woof! Woof!"

BUTCHERS

I don't know why they call it take-home pay.
I can never get it past the butcher.

Do you know what they're charging for a steak these days? In our neighborhood the kids don't play Cops and Robbers anymore. They play Cops and Butchers.

And if you want to know why they're called butchers, look what they do to your budget!

They take advantage of women. I told my wife, "This morning I went in to our butcher. I said, 'Let's stop this nonsense. I want something that's lean, red, tender, and it shouldn't cost more than a dollar a pound!'" My wife said, "What did he give you?" I said, "Raspberry Jell-O."

That's the thing to be today—a butcher. A butcher shop is where steaks, pork chops, lamb chops, and customers get trimmed. . . . Not necessarily in that order.

There's a new game called Butcher's Roulette. You take your life savings and you're given the names of six different butcher shops—and one of them is open.

One butcher went to a psychiatrist. He said he was afraid of height. The doctor cured him just like that [SNAP YOUR FINGERS]! Told him not to sit on his wallet.

The saddest story I ever heard was about a butcher who wanted to become a brain surgeon but he couldn't afford the cut in pay.

It's incredible. The butchers claim they're not making any money. The wholesalers claim they're not making any money. The ranchers claim they're not making any money. So who's making the money? Sometimes I get the uneasy feeling that somewhere there are cows buying mutual funds!

Have you checked out the price of beef lately?
If anybody says, "Holy cow!"—you better believe it!

Do you know they're charging two dollars a pound for ribs?
I wouldn't pay two dollars a pound for ribs if they were attached to Raquel Welch!

I'll tell you how high meat prices are.
Even plumbers are beginning to notice.

Meat prices are so high, I'm on a very special kind of diet. I go to the butcher shop and eat my heart out!

Did you hear what happened down the street? A housewife walked in and robbed a butcher! There's a switch.

The dictionary has a new definition for beef. That's what you do when the butcher tells you the price.

Unfortunately, we have a butcher who likes to rub it in. I mean, I don't mind his wearing a diamond ring. I don't even mind his smoking two-dollar cigars. It's that mink apron that gets to me!

I'm so naïve. Up until I met this butcher, I never knew Rolls-Royce made a delivery truck.

He doesn't even try to sell you the good cuts of meat anymore. For the last six months the thickest thing he's put on the scale is his thumb!

My wife's a weight watcher. With our butcher you have to be.

My butcher has a very interesting scale.
Yesterday a fly landed on it—4½ pounds!

You know you're in trouble when the butcher puts the wax paper on
the scale and that alone weighs thirty-eight cents!

CAMPING

Show me a voice crying in the wilderness and I'll show you a camper
who forgot the booze.

You think I'm kidding? I've found that most campers fall into two
categories—the backpackers and the six-packers!

Did you hear about the campground that was raided because of a six-
pack? Three couples in a sleeping bag.

For those of you who have never gone camping, let me explain it this
way: Camping is when you go into the woods and enjoy all the
things that if they happened to you at home you'd complain about!

Do you know that camping attracts 24 million every year?
Not people—mosquitoes.

And if it isn't mosquitoes, it's moths or bees or hornets or chiggers.
There isn't a camper alive who doesn't wish that when the two
chiggers crawled side by side into the ark—Noah had gone [STAMP
YOUR FOOT ON THE FLOOR]!

Believe me, it isn't easy being a camper. You don't know what fear is
until you've zipped up your sleeping bag—and the itch on your big
toe starts to move!

I don't mind the bugs with two legs. I don't mind the bugs with four
legs. I don't even mind the bugs with six legs. But when they start
looking like the Rockettes—forget it!

CAR REPAIRS

Owning a car wouldn't be half so expensive if it wasn't for two things—parts and labor.

I think all auto mechanics go to the same school—Shaft U.

Let's face it, to you it may be your motor that's knocking. To a mechanic, it's opportunity!

Actually, they don't call them mechanics anymore. Automotive diagnosticians! They've got the white gown; the three buttons on the shoulder; "Don't touch me—I'm sterile!"

These fellas have so much authority; so much poise; so much dignity—it almost makes you proud to have their fingerprints on your seat covers!

They charged me $87 for parts and $350 for labor. I said, "Whose labor?" He said, "My wife's. We just had another kid."

I couldn't believe this bill. The smallest thing on it was the telephone number!

Did you hear about the automobile mechanic who bought a hospital and he's making a fortune? If you bring in your wife for an operation, they give you a loaner.

It isn't easy being an automobile mechanic. Let's face it, how would you like to stand in the middle of a garage knowing that every car that comes through that door is defective?

I have a great auto insurance policy. If my car is in an accident and it's a total loss, the company pays in full—for the stamp it puts on the letter that cancels my coverage.

Progress is like this. In 1931 you ran into someone and it cost you $50 to have him fixed up. Now you run into someone and it costs you $500 to have the bumper fixed up.

Paying the repair bills on a used car is a case of a lemon putting the squeeze on you!

CARS

The automobile is really in trouble. Engineers want to eliminate the steering column, ecologists want to eliminate the engine, and Planned Parenthood wants to eliminate the back seat.

Dear Ralph Nader: Normally I don't get uptight about things like a car, but yesterday my wife said she was going home to Mother—and it wouldn't start.

I think somebody's trying to steal my car.
I see two men pushing it up the street!

I just paid for my automobile insurance and it's a little ridiculous. I had to sell my car to do it!

I drove coast-to-coast in one of those subcompacts that get thirty-five miles to a gallon, and it was really embarrassing. I had to stop at three more gas stations than *it* did!

There are two ways to get your car clean and shiny. The five-minute car wash is when machines do it. Then there's the five-month car wash. That's when you ask your kids to do it.

Sometimes I get the feeling my car was produced in Detroit—by mess production.

I'll tell you what kind of a car I've got. You know how some people use Simoniz on their car? I use lemon wax.

It's the kind of a car you have to keep moving. The minute you stop, people think it's an accident!

In all fairness, this car does go forty-three miles on a gallon. Forty-three miles on a gallon! It gets towed a lot.

CARS (NEW)

You can always tell an experienced car buyer by one thing. They always pick a dealer within walking distance of their home.

I'll tell you what the new cars are like. I've got a '79 that was recalled to Detroit—and it couldn't make it!

Have you seen the 1980 cars? They really look like they can get you where you're going—the poorhouse.

The 1980 cars are a fantastic leap forward in technological achievement. One item alone boggles the imagination—the power tissue dispenser!

Personally, there's only one thing I want to see in a 1980 car—me!

Do you know they charge $400 for a power seat so you can see over the steering wheel? It's ridiculous. I got the same thing and it only cost me a buck and a half—elevator shorts!

When buying a new car, you should always use the A.A.A. technique. The first three prices they give you, you say, "Eh?" [CUPPING YOUR HAND TO YOUR EAR].

I bought a new car and right away I had good news and bad news. The good news is that it has something that can withstand damage at up to five miles an hour. The bad news is—it's the tires.

I'll tell you how thin these tires are: Some drivers worry about nails. I worry about mosquitoes.

You know how some cars come with a warranty?
This comes with a tow truck.

I bought this car because the salesman said it was great on gas.
It should be great—it only has one cylinder.
It goes from zero to sixty in eleven days.

You know how with some cars, you want to gun the engine? With this one, it's the guy who sold it to you!

This car is so slow, dogs don't chase it. They catch it!

Never buy a cheap car. Yesterday a pigeon flew·over mine. Cost me seventy-five dollars to get out the dent.

The salesman said, "Now we have this model in eggshell." I said, "I know about the fenders. Tell me about the color."

The workmanship really isn't in cars these days. I just saw a bumper marked FRAGILE!

Detroit has come up with a bumper that can absorb an impact at five miles an hour. That takes care of nearsighted joggers—now what about cars?

Isn't that a wonderful concept—a five-mile-an-hour bumper? Sounds like an elderly stripper.

I love the way they give you a warranty on a new car for twelve months. The only thing I've ever had on a car that lasted for twelve months is aggravation.

Have you noticed how the new cars all seem to have two things that are factory-installed? Air conditioning and defects.

There's one thing I can never understand about the new cars. Why do they make them so low to the ground? Yesterday I stuck out my hand to make a left turn and I'll never forget it. Neither will that cop tying his shoelace!

CARS (USED)

My car was formerly owned by a little old lady from Pasadena. I think it was this car that aged her.

The nice part about buying a used car is, you don't have to worry about changing the oil every two thousand miles—because there's never any left!

I won't say how far the mileage has been turned back, but the speedometer is in Roman numerals.

The salesman said this car has a lot of interesting little touches. I think the proper word is "dents."

CHESS

Chess is a game that requires intense concentration and absolute silence. During one game, a player sneezed and his opponent said, "Gesundheit." The first player said, "Did you come here to play or talk?"

It doesn't make sense, like a chess team with a cheerleader.

Chess is a game in which people sit for hours, staring ahead, not moving a muscle. We have the same thing in Washington. It's called Civil Service.

My daughter is interested in chess. Last night I heard her saying to her boyfriend, "When are you going to make your move?" I *hope* she's interested in chess.

My wife's hairdresser hates chess. He won't have anything to do with a game where a queen is expendable.

CHILDREN

Fortunately, I have rather tolerant kids. They just look on me as the square in the family circle.

If you're a parent, you know that 1959 was a great year for wine, not kids.

Tonight I'd like to say a kind word about kids. Do you realize, if you have kids, you don't have to hold up a seashell to hear a roar?

Raising kids is like eating grapefruit. No matter how you do it, the little squirts get to you.

Some parents get so upset with their kids, they kick the bucket. That's where they make a big mistake. Leave the bucket alone. Kick the kids!

Let your kids know that you think about them occasionally. Grit your teeth!

I feel sorry for people who don't have kids. I really do. Whenever there's a discussion about Excedrin headaches, they just stand there like dum-dums!

It's a little frustrating to hear a kid who's already cost you $22,000 say his prayers—and you get mentioned ahead of the goldfish but after the gerbil.

I know this sounds kinda sentimental, but every night after dinner, I spend what I call the Children's Hour. I wait for them to get off the phone.

What my kids don't know about thrift would fill a bankbook.

My kids have lost so many teeth, we have the only budget in town where the tooth fairy comes after rent!

Every time I see the Statue of Liberty, I think of my kids. She has a book in her hand but I've never seen it open.

Years ago kids lived a hand-to-mouth existence.
Every time they opened their mouth, they got a hand right across it.

My mother raised us tennis style.
You've never seen such a backhand!

Five-year-olds really know how to live.
They eat, drink, and make messy!

I guess I shouldn't complain. I know a couple who have five kids, two dogs, and a cat. Last year their house was vandalized three times before they discovered it.

Kids are so deflatable. One little kid came up to me and said, "I'm the greatest counter on the block. I'm the greatest counter in the city. I'm the greatest counter in the world! 1—2—3." I said, "Go on." He said, "There's more?"

Have you noticed how many kids are allergic to sheets? The minute they have to slide between them, they break out in tantrums!

We have a problem with our kids. They get ten hours of sleep a day. At night, nothing!

This kid's eyes are so red, maybe you saw him.
Last year he was poster boy for Murine!

We're getting desperate. You know what we gave him for dinner last night? French-fried Sominex!

CHINA

Do you know there are now 950 million Chinese? It's incredible. Doesn't anybody ever have a headache?

Personally, I don't trust China. Any country that has 950 million people and claims table tennis is their favorite indoor sport—will lie about other things too.

Chinese and Americans have a lot in common. For instance, the Chinese read from right to left. So do Americans, looking at menus.

No wonder the Chinese don't get along with the Russians.
You ever try to eat borscht with chopsticks?

I don't want to brag but my wife happens to be a China watcher. Every time I dry the dishes.

CHRISTMAS

Christmas has a wonderful message. It's better to give than to receive. Internal Revenue has that same message.

I'm really worried about the commercialization of Christmas. Nowadays the only time you hear someone mention God is when they stick their finger in a Christmas light socket.

Lincoln said you can't fool all of the people all the time. Lincoln never read the instructions for assembling Christmas toys!

The government is getting after firms that make dangerous toys. You'd be surprised how many toys have things on them that can hurt you—like the price tag.

The most unbelievable thing about Christmas is that poem about children hanging their stockings by the chimney with care. We live in an apartment—no chimney. Nowadays who owns stockings, and when have you ever heard of a kid hanging something up?

We have two kids and they're always arguing. Like last Christmas one of them wanted a cat and the other wanted a dog. So we compromised. We got a cat and taught it how to bark.

It's all in the way you look at it. To us he's Rudolph, the Red-Nosed Reindeer. To Dancer, Prancer, Donder, and Blitzen—he's a wino!

You know what shakes me? Those fruit cakes made with brandy, rum, and whiskey! How do you come in at three o'clock in the morning and tell your wife you've had one slice too many?

I know a fella who came home from the Christmas office party and he's in terrible trouble. His wife found lipstick on his collar . . . bone.

A truly religious person is someone who can find a spiritual message in a trombone solo of "Silent Night."

On the eighty-third day after Christmas my true love sent to me—bills!

CHRISTMAS PRESENTS

Every time I go Christmas shopping, I know three things are going to give out on me—money, patience, and feet!

If you're working on your Christmas shopping list, for the millionaire who has everything: a sauna that's air-conditioned!

For janitors, doormen, and elevator operators, this is a tiptop time of the year. If you don't tip, they blow their top.

I got the perfect Christmas present for my doctor.
A nurse who knows how to caddy!

Happiness is that brief glorious moment between the time your wife says she's going to get you a hookah for Christmas—and when you realize that's a Turkish pipe.

My wife always gives me strange things for Christmas—like a bath towel that says DRY-CLEAN ONLY.

Guess what I got for my wife? Perfume! But never again. I went up to the salesgirl and I said, "What kind of perfume do you have?" She said, "We have FINE AT NINE—GREAT AT EIGHT—and HEAVEN AT SEVEN." I said, "HEAVEN AT SEVEN? Lady, we've been married for twenty-six years." She said, "How about NIX AT SIX?"

You know the easiest way to avoid arguments with your wife at Christmastime? Promise her anything—and give it to her!

And with all these fancy bottles they're putting liquor in, you really have to be careful. Like yesterday I poured myself an Arpège and soda!

All I want for Christmas is for my kids to hang up three things—stockings, mistletoe, and the phone!

CHRISTMAS (SANTA CLAUS)

Every Christmas we get a visit from the jolly gent with the great big bag over his shoulder. It's my son home from college and the great big bag is laundry.

I think we should be very grateful to Santa Claus. He's the only one who comes from overseas and gives instead of takes.

Santa Claus and Uncle Sam have a lot in common. They both leave goodies all over the world and wind up holding the bag.

If you look at the labels on toys this year, you realize Santa Claus is no longer at the North Pole. He's in Hong Kong!

We know an old maid who still believes in Santa Claus—and anything else that lets her climb onto a man's lap.

Fathers rise to great heights during the Christmas season. A father and his little daughter were standing in front of a department-store Santa Claus and he was saying, "Yes, Virginia, this is Santa Claus—and that was Santa Claus in Macy's, and that was Santa Claus in Gimbel's, and that was Santa Claus on the street corner." His daughter said, "How can there be so many Santa Clauses?" He turned to the fella in the big red suit and said, "Santa, tell Virginia how you fell into the Xerox machine!"

Christmas in California is fascinating. Where else can you hear a department-store Santa Claus saying, "Don't sit on my knee. It's sunburned!"

My brother-in-law is a street-corner Santa Claus. He isn't too bright but they did give him a sheet of instructions. In fact, this morning I was watching him work. He went: "Ho! Ho!" [LOOK DOWN AS IF READING INSTRUCTIONS] "Ho!"

Did you hear about the department-store Santa Claus who suffers from water on the knee—sometimes six or seven times a day?

This is the time of year when all parents tell their kids they'd better be good or Santa Claus won't stop at their house. It's called a Christmas club.

My wife is very good about Christmas. A department-store Santa Claus asked me what I wanted. I said, "A twenty-one-year-old blond sexpot." And my wife said I'm gonna get it!

CHRISTMAS TREES

I passed one of those lots that sell Christmas trees. You know the kind. They're dedicated to the proposition that only God can make a tree and only man can make a buck!

Wait'll you see what they're getting for Christmas trees this year. For the first time in history, you're giving them more green than they're giving you!

You should have seen the tree we wound up with. We paid twelve dollars for a tree that's so small, I think it was planted in Israel—by Arabs!

This tree was so puny, three passersby sneered at it—and two of them were dogs!

I always feel guilty about an aluminum Christmas tree until I hear a fire truck go by.

CHURCH

Volunteer work is when you have to explain to your kids that Daddy hasn't died. He just became president of his church.

As the head of any church board of trustees will tell you, after all is said and done, there's a lot more said than done.

You hear some fascinating conversations on Sunday mornings. For instance: "I didn't say he was cheap. I just said he was late for church because he had to change something." "A tire?" "No. A dollar bill."

I'm always suspicious of any church that tells you the end is near— and then asks you to sign a three-year Building Fund pledge.

You can always tell a church that isn't doing well.
The Cadillac they raffle off is used.

I go to a Congregational church that's so democratic, last week the minister said, "O Lord, we ask Thy forgiveness—48 to 33 with 12 abstentions!"

One church is so progressive, it's doing a modernized version of the Christmas story. The three Wise Men are bringing gift certificates!

I could tell it was a progressive church when we all stood up to sing the first hymn—"Fine and Dandy."

But you haven't lived until you've gone to church in Detroit. Where else can you find bucket pews?

The minister asked me, "Are you a soldier in the Army of the Lord?" I said, "Yes I am." He said, "Then why do we only see you at Christmas and Easter?" I said, "I'm in the Secret Service."

What a wonderful motto for a German fundamentalist church: YOU BETTER BELIEVE IT!

CITY LIFE

Nowadays when you live in the heart of the city, you start thinking about a transplant.

I come from a town where the city officials are so crooked, the Mafia is the reform group!

I think this city has finally achieved the goal of a classless society. I've never seen so many people with no class!

This city is really desperate for money. I just saw a coin-operated fire alarm.

It costs you about the same to live in cities as it does in the suburbs. What you save on carfare you spend on locks.

I had a terrible thing happen to me yesterday. Opportunity knocked on my door—and by the time I unhooked the chain, pushed back the bolt, turned the two locks, and shut off the burglar alarm—it was gone!

This is the only city I know where you figure muggings into your budget!

In this city you don't walk for your health—you run!

There was a riot this morning at the city jail. The prisoners said the food was terrible. Then they broke down the door—with a sausage.

I'll say one thing for this town: It has a very religious Sanitation Department. They only take up a collection once a week.

I don't ask for much out of life. I just want to live in a city where the garbage is collected at least as often as the taxes.

Yesterday the head of our Highway Department said he's very aware of the condition of our streets. In fact, he was personally going right out to fill eighteen holes. Then he picked up his golf clubs and left.

Life is so unfair. If you come across on the *Mayflower*, you're honored. If you come across on Forty-seventh Street, you're arrested.

I stepped out of my hotel and right away I met a girl who was mentioned three times in one of the greatest war songs every written: "Tramp, Tramp, Tramp, the Boys Are Marching!"

I won't say what some of these girls look like, but if someone puts an arm around you—you hope it's a mugger!

CLEANLINESS

I've found that cleanliness is next to godliness—but in a six-year-old, it's next to impossible.

It's very discouraging. We have a six-year-old and the only four-letter word he doesn't know is "soap"!

I mean, it's one thing to be dirty but this kid has a belly button you could grow mushrooms in!

When he says he can't hear too well, we don't take him to an ear doctor. Roto-Rooter!

There's no question about it, we have a problem. You can tell that by the three different kinds of soap we have in our bathroom—Lux for my wife, Dial for me, and Brillo for him!

Have you ever tried to give a six-year-old a bath? Sometimes I think the dirt is tattooed on!

And there are always telltale little signs when your kid isn't taking enough baths. Like, he has the only bathrobe in town that gets dirty from the inside.

We try to bribe him to take baths. One time we got him three toy boats. I won't say what the water looked like when he was through, but two of them went aground!

They gave an aptitude test in school and it really worries us. Sixteen kids were best suited to be a doctor. Twelve kids were best suited to be a lawyer. Eight kids were best suited to be an accountant. And he was best suited to be a swamp!

You know how some parents pin a kid's mittens to his coat? We also pin something to his coat—Airwick!

Unfortunately, the kid has answers. One time I said, "Why can't you be like Daddy and wash all that nasty dirt off your face?" He said, "I'd rather be like Mommy and cover it up with powder!"

The greatest problem facing the American family today can be summed up in six words: Ovens are self-cleaning and kids aren't!

Kids really stick together. If you took a bath once a month, you'd be a little gummy too!

CLOSINGS

I have one favor to ask. For the last three weeks I've been practicing this speech in front of my dog. So if you want to make me feel at home, when I get to the finish, please don't applaud. Just bark!

In conclusion, let's all join together in singing the last stanza of: "I'll Never Forget Sally Standing Aghast, As Her Panty Hose Slowly Sank to Half-mast!"

I have to be going now. I placed an order for twenty dollars' worth of groceries and I want to be home when they slip it under the door.

And so, in closing, let me leave you with three phrases that, more than any others, sum up the spirit of the Christmas season: PEACE ON EARTH, GOODWILL TO ALL MEN, and BATTERIES NOT INCLUDED!

And so in closing, let me leave you with the words of that famous horticulturist Luther Burbank, who said: "Never look down on a lily. Tomorrow that lily may be looking down on you!"

I leave you with this thought: LOVE THY NEIGHBOR. But remember to draw the blinds first.

CONVENTION CLOSING: And so, as we head home with faith in our hearts, information in our minds, bills in our pockets, and towels in our luggage . . .

ADJOURNMENT: And now, in the immortal words of Brigadier General George Armstrong Custer: "Let's get the hell out of here!"

CLOTHING

There's so much trouble in the world. Yesterday a five-year-old kid was in a department store with his mother and she said, "Hang on to my skirt." The kid got a hernia from reaching.

Everybody likes to put on airs. I have an uncle who introduces himself as a man of the cloth. Big deal—he's a tailor!

I go to one of those neighborhood clothing stores that has an answer for everything. If you like a suit that's half a size too large, they don't alter it. They buy you two pizzas and a malted!

Everything you buy today is imported. Look at this shirt. You know what the washing instructions were? "First—find a flat rock!"

I had a forty-two-dollar suit made in Hong Kong and it's just great—once you get used to the diagonal zipper.

Forty-two dollars and it's custom-tailored. I custom every time I wear it.

I like that suit. Who's your tailor—Dear Shabby?

Our daughter is learning dressmaking. Last week she cut out a dress pattern on the floor. She wound up with two dresses. One silk and one broadloom.

My daughter had a very embarrassing experience Saturday night. She went to a party and someone else was wearing the very same outfit she was—her date.

More and more we're beginning to look like the civilization of ancient Egypt. You can't tell the daddies from the mummies.

I'm not going to say anything about the way kids look these days. Bum's the word!

I saw a kid going to school this morning wearing an undershirt, blue jeans, no socks, and no shoes. My mother wouldn't have let me leave the house like that if it was on fire!

I just figured out why so many kids wear sandals.
So they can count up to twenty.

My wife has one pantsuit with big brass buttons down the front, and every night I have this same nightmare—that I'm arrested for molesting a cop!

My wife wears support stockings that are so good, she's the only woman I know who can faint standing up!

Girls, every time you get a run in one leg of your panty hose, cut off the leg with the run in it and save the panty hose. Eventually, you will have a set of panty hose with one good right leg and another set with one good left leg. Put them both on, one over the other, and you'll have a perfectly good pair of panty hose! It's efficient; it's economical; and it confuses the hell out of sex maniacs!

My wife has one outfit that's so sexy we can only send it to a mature dry cleaner.

COLLEGE

I complain about kids a lot, but when my oldest son leaves for college in the fall, he'll leave an emptiness behind him. It'll be in our savings account.

Behind every kid who completes four years of college there stand two parents who are also graduating—magna cum bankrupt.

It's $115 a credit and that doesn't include books. Do you know that some college books cost as much as $25? The last time I paid $25 for a book, I had to worry about Customs finding it!

Last week he brought home a new textbook. It has a wonderful title: *Proper English for You and I.*

Nowadays there is only one sure way to get a decent high school education—go to college!

My son is a senior in college. I don't know what they're teaching him, but yesterday we were all sitting around the dinner table. My wife turns to me and says, "I sure hope he G-R-A-D-U-A-T-E-S!"

I don't want to start any trouble, but have you noticed what kids are handed during their graduation ceremony? Dummy diplomas!

I heard two parents talking and one said, "My son took eight years to go through college. He's a D.D." The other parent said, "A doctor of divinity?" He said, "No. A dum-dum!"

And I just got a phone call from my daughter: "What's that? You're calling from college and you're pregnant. How did that happen? He told you it was perfectly safe. Why was it perfectly safe? 'Cause the stork flies South for the winter."

Kids study psychology to learn about anger, hostility, rejection, indifference, and all the other things their parents have learned from *them.*

COLLEGE ADMISSIONS

I'm really worried about the lowering of standards in American education. I can remember when if a high school student wanted to go to college, the admitting office would take his qualifications. Now they take his pulse.

Today, to get into a good college you have to satisfy its SAT requirements. If you SAT in a high school for four years, you're in!

They're letting kids into college who don't even know how to write. For instance, they admitted one girl because she made straight A's. The B's she got a little crooked.

You can tell the colleges are lowering their standards. One kid took an aptitude test and he was stuck on the very first question. It said: "NAME?"

It kinda shakes you up to ask a senior the time and he says, "Wait a minute. I'll look at my ticktock."

Did you hear about the speech major who was rejected by the college of her cherce?

My daughter picked a wonderful college to go to. It's in Massachusetts just a little outside of our budget.

She went about picking the school in a very serious way. She got this big fat book listing all the schools. She studied it. She wrote to twenty-three different colleges; applied to eight of them; visited five of them; and finally chose the one school that offered her the most of what she was interested in—boys.

My daughter went to one of those progressive colleges. She picked her own subjects, her own books, her own teachers, she never took any tests, and today she's living in a $90,000 house! Mine—who'll give her a job?

COMPETITION

We can all profit by mistakes—particularly if our competition makes enough of them.

Our competition makes so many mistakes, there are three baskets on every desk: IN, OUT, and OOOPS!

I happen to know that my competitor's secretary loves to go to the racetrack and sit in front of the starting gate. It's the only chance she gets to see a horse's front!

I had a wonderful thing happen today. A cop was chasing a pickpocket, yelling, "Stop, thief!" And three of my competitors turned around.

I'll say one thing for our competitors: They know a good thing when they see it. That's why they're always writing for our catalog.

No, I'm only kidding. We have very fine upstanding competitors. The reason they're upstanding is they just had their furniture repossessed.

COMPUTERS

I think the boss is trying to replace me.
He's looking for a computer that grovels.

What this world really needs is something to put human beings back in the running again. Like a dumb computer!

I'll tell you how human machines have become. I know an electronic brain that only thinks of one thing—naked computers!

Then there's the girl who went to a computer dating service and said, "I want to meet somebody who's six feet six, strong, fears no one, and who'll bite me on the ear." So they introduced her to an alligator.

CONSERVATION

Conservationists are people who pour trouble on oiled waters!

There are three reasons for being a conservationist.
(1) You will help prevent the destruction of the world as you know it.
(2) You will save hundreds of endangered species from extermination. And
(3) You'll finally have a reason not to buy your wife a fur coat.

At the last count 180 million trees have been cut down to provide paper for books that warn us about wasting our natural resources.

We have some of the most beautiful wilderness areas in the world. Unfortunately the people who dig them the most have bulldozers.

If we keep wasting our natural resources, 1984 will be something like this: A family gets up early in the morning and the father says,

"June 24th! Isn't it great? Our day to go up to the Berkshires and look at the tree."

I'll get enthused about recycled paper when they can make trees out of it.

The ecologists want us to return our empties to the supermarket. I brought back six beer bottles and my wallet.

Have you noticed how, no matter where you go, you can't get away from empty beer cans? Some people think the world is going to end with a bang. Some people think it's going to end with a whimper. I think it's going to end with a burp!

Just look at what we're doing to the environment. I can remember when we TIPTOED THROUGH THE TULIPS. Now we FLITTER THROUGH THE LITTER!

Recycling is when you use the same thing over and over again. In television it's jokes.

If you think "recycle" is a fancy word, I just met a textile reclamation engineer. He's a ragpicker!

CONSUMERISM

Misery is spending $350,000 to bring out a brand-new product and your first customer is Ralph Nader.

You know how Ralph Nader is always investigating things that can hurt you? I just sent him a copy of my income tax return!

You have to give Ralph Nader credit for dedication.
Yesterday I saw him buying a Five Day Deodorant Pad and a calendar.

I'll tell you what kind of a world we're living in. I just saw a lifetime pen that's guaranteed for three months!

I just found out what they mean by POPULAR MECHANICS. They're the ones whose bills match their estimates!

I love to read *Popular Mechanics*. It's one of the few magazines you can buy where if you see something that's stripped, it's gears!

CONVENTIONS

Business shows are all alike—you big-mouth your prospects and poor-mouth your suppliers.

I just came from one of those warm, friendly, cooperative conventions that feature give and take. Everybody was trying to give discounts and take customers.

They're playing a wonderful new game at this convention. It's called salesman's roulette. You sell a huge order to one of six firms. Five are going into textiles [ADAPT TO YOUR FIELD] and one is going into Chapter Eleven.

I had to stop bringing my assistant to conventions. It was too embarrassing. Who orders beer on the rocks?

This is my kind of group—a Beef Stew Convention. The salesmen are all beefing and the prospects are all stewed.

I spent the whole afternoon in our hospitality suite. I've drunk to the health of so many customers, I'm beginning to lose my own!

And have you noticed how the bartenders in hospitality suites really pour it out? I had a drink that was so strong, instead of a cocktail napkin, it came with a get-well card.

Fortunately we have a rule at this convention.
Any order for $3 million that's signed with a swizzle stick is null and void.

I won't say there's been a lot of drinking going on, but a rather disturbing thing happened on the sixteenth floor last night. A very loud party was thrown across the hall. I was the party.

I know a lot of wives think that conventions are nothing but wine, women, and song, but that's not true. Not once have I heard one of you fellas singing.

They said there would be a lot of surprises at this convention, and there have been—even if you don't count the prices at the hotel coffee shop. . . . Believe me, there are no atheists in the hotel coffee shop. All you have to do is look at a menu and you say, "Good God!"

This morning the waitress brought me a cup of coffee, a glass of orange juice, and a doughnut—$2.75! It's incredible. In some cities, the muggers wear masks. Here they wear aprons!

But I'll say one thing for that glass of orange juice. They took out all the pits in it. They had to. If they left them in, there wouldn't have been room for the juice!

No, I'm only kidding. It's a wonderful place. Any coffee shop that can make the *Fortune* 500 deserves respect.

And to all you fellas who have come to this convention without your wives—don't worry. I happen to know the waiters mix.

It really was a very exciting convention. Looked like the finals for the Olympic yawning team.

It's really a shame. There was one dirty old man at the convention and even he was over the hill. I heard a girl saying to him, "Oh, you're only interested in one thing." Then she had to tell him what it was.

COOKING

Our neighborhood massage parlor must serve fantastic food. All the truck drivers go there.

"The way to a man's heart is through his stomach!" I'll tell you who said that. My son, who is now in his ninth year in medical school.

I wonder if Julia Child's husband has ever looked up from the dinner table and said, "*Petits chaussons au Roquefort? Potage Parmentier? Filets de poisson pochés au vin blanc? Haricots verts à la crème? Endives à la Flamande* and *tarte Normande aux pommes?* We had that last night!"

Our neighbor happens to be an authority on Ancient Greece. Never cleans the oven!

I wouldn't tell my wife this—but I'm just as glad when she doesn't make breakfast. She makes a lousy martini.

When it comes to meals, we either eat out or order in. In our house we have two things that are always cold—the refrigerator and the stove!

My wife is a Colonel Sanders junkie. That's right. We've been married five years and she still doesn't know where the kitchen is.

She's one of those modern cooks. Her favorite recipe is "heat and serve."

I've eaten so much frozen food, I have the only tonsils in town that are chapped!

And she has a thing about keeping leftovers. She loves to keep leftovers. We've been married twenty years now and our garbage can is brand-new!

Does my wife save leftovers? Yesterday we had a fourteen-pound meat loaf!

Every time I open the refrigerator I see two dozen little dishes of food—shivering. It's embarrassing. Have you ever said, "Gesundheit!" to succotash?

We have an autumn leaves refrigerator. You look inside and everything is turning.

At any given moment our refrigerator has three things that are green —spinach, parsley, and bread.

You should see our bread. It comes in three different flavors—white, rye, and Roquefort.

And I don't mind telling you, I'm getting a little suspicious of some of these leftovers. Yesterday she brought out a chicken wearing a Willkie button!

And she's always starting trouble. Yesterday she said, "We are what we eat!" I know that sounds innocent enough, but I happened to have a handful of nuts at the time.

There's a chef at the Pentagon who has everybody uptight. He keeps spilling the beans.

CREDIT

Life was a lot simpler when what was honored was Father and Mother rather than all major credit cards.

We buy everything on credit. That's right. We have the only toilet water in town labeled OWE DE COLOGNE.

I won't say what our credit is like, but if you look us up in Bradstreet, we're Dun!

I had a wonderful thing happen this morning. A fella knocked on the door and I said, "Who is it?" He said, "A bill collector." So I gave him the stack on my desk.

And when you're behind in your bills, you always pay the creditor who yells the loudest. That's right. From force of habit I write, "Pay to the holler of . . ."

A supplier called me up to say my account was delinquent. What do I care if it stays out late?

Some firms are so unreasonable. One of our suppliers got mad because we took three days to pay a bill. Christmas, Easter, and the Fourth of July.

CRIME

Crime doesn't pay! But at least it doesn't tell you the check is in the mail.

Criminals are so brazen these days, I was in a department store and saw a guy trying on nylons over his head.

Crime in the streets is getting to be such a problem, yesterday Clark Kent went into a phone booth—and stayed there!

Remember when it was Superman who was faster than a speeding bullet? Now it's anybody who gets out of Central Park.

Taking a walk in this town is like playing baseball. The hardest part is getting home safe!

I'll tell you how bad the crime problem has become. Yesterday I heard two people calling for help—and they were muggers!

Sure this city has its problems, but I like the way people still stand tall in the streets. You'd stand tall, too, if you had to keep your money in your shoes!

They now have an organization called [YOUR TOWN] Anonymous. Every time you get to thinking the crime situation isn't so bad, you call them up; they send someone over—and he never makes it!

I'll tell you how much crime they have in this town. They don't have an electric chair. They have an electric couch!

I live in a very religious neighborhood. One time I said to a priest, "Is it true that in this neighborhood, if you carry a cross, you never have to worry?" He said, "Yes. But it all depends on how fast you carry it!"

Crime is so bad in my neighborhood, I heard a delicatessen owner say he's putting locks on his bagels!

But you'll have no trouble with crime in this town if you follow four simple suggestions:
(1) Your door should be steel-backed.
(2) Your door should have a hidden peephole.
(3) Your door should have a heavy-duty, pick-proof lock. And
(4) Your door should be moved to Bangor, Maine.

DANCE SCHOOLS

I went to one of those dance schools that advertise "25 LESSONS FOR $5" and in the very first lesson I learned something—that it wasn't going to cost $5.

Have you ever been to a dance school? I walked in the door and right away this voluptuous instructor came over and put her hand on a rather intimate place—my wallet.

They tried to sign me up for a twenty-year course in social dancing. I said, "Twenty years? What if I don't live twenty years?" That's when they showed me the casket with the phonograph.

But it's a lot of fun. You'd be amazed how many old codgers are taking dance lessons. It's the only way they can back a girl up and not have to follow through!

DATING

Pardon me, miss. I don't ordinarily talk to strange women on the street—but I'm on my way to confession and I'm short of material.

Love is so confusing. You tell a girl she looks great and then what's the first thing you do? Turn out the lights!

Remember when a fella took a girl out and it was a big deal to get a good-night kiss? Now that's like the breadsticks at an Italian dinner.

Romance is kissing your girl friend on the eyes.
Reality is getting her false eyelashes caught in your teeth!

As I understand it, smoking is hazardous to your health, drinking is bad for your liver, and sex is responsible for overpopulation. I went out with a girl last night and we chewed gum till three in the morning.

Don't you just hate it when a company makes claims it can't deliver? I bought that gasoline that eliminates stalling—parked with my girl. It doesn't work.

I said, "Do you want to fool around?"
She said, "I'll have you know I shrink from any immoral behavior!"
And she did. She was four feet six inches high!

Parking with a girl in Lover's Lane can be a traumatic experience. I mean, how do you explain to the AAA how she got her foot caught in the window?

I know a girl who wears her heart on her sleeve.
I told you those transplants weren't perfected.

Ask any girl and she'll tell you why they're called swinging singles bars. 'Cause that's all anybody spends.

DAUGHTERS

I've got a daughter who's a junkie.
If you don't believe it, I'll show you her room.

It's ridiculous. We paid $300 for wall-to-wall carpeting.
Haven't seen it in five years!

I'll tell you what her room looks like—
we have roaches that beg for Raid!

It's all right to be a little sloppy, but the walls haven't been cleaned in two years. We have molding that is!

If it's true we come from dust,
under the bed alone is the birth of a nation!

I have one of those Vincent van Gogh teenagers.
She only listens to me with one ear.

Teenagers are great. One time a kid knocked on the door and he said, "My name is Stanley. S for Sophisticated, T for Terrific, A for Attractive, N for Nice, L for Loaded, E for Experienced, and Y for Yummy! Is your daughter home?" I said, "Who cares? Kiss me!"

My daughter has no luck at all. Last year a fella asked if he could change her name to his and she said yes. And ever since he's been calling her Melvin.

You should see some of the characters my daughter goes out with. She brings home so many crumbs, I don't know whether to worry about her or cockroaches.

Times have really changed. Twenty years ago, if someone asked you, "What has long hair, smells, and follows your daughter around?" it'd be her dog. Now it's her boyfriend!

Show me a fella who has four teenage daughters and one bathroom —and I'll show you a dirty old man!

I just had a terrible experience. My daughter said she was joining the subculture. I said, "Forget it! No kid of mine is gonna work on a U-boat!"

DEEJAY LINES

This is [YOUR NAME]—the eyes, ears, nose, and big mouth of [YOUR TOWN]!

My name is _____. Not that anyone's interested but it does let my wife know I got here all right.

I understand they just got back from a record-breaking tour. Every time somebody heard them sing, they went out and broke their records.

I once worked on a station that played nothing but country and western. You've heard of the Top Forty? This was the North Forty.

I used to work in a station that was so poor, our time checks bounced!

This happens to be a very progressive station. Next week we're going to put a radio in a car and give traffic reports to helicopters!

I had a terrible thing happen to me this morning. I heard a mother say to her six-year-old kid, "Do you want to hear the '[YOUR NAME] Show'?" He said, "No." And she said, "Then behave yourself!"

I don't want to brag, but this is one show that has a lot of fans. We can't afford air conditioning.

A little song dedicated to the world today: "I've got a right to sing the blues; I just tuned in the Ten O'Clock News."

That was "You Always Hurt the One You Love," and I'd like to dedicate it to my wife—the only woman in history with switchblade toenails!

I know a sheet music printer who went broke because of a typographical error. He ran off two million copies of "Pig of My Heart."

Next we have a song that describes why I never worry about what to get my wife for her birthday. It's called:
"Someday My Hints Will Come."

That was: "I Lost My Contact Lenses" or
             "I Wonder Who's Kissing Me Now?"

AFTER A WILD RECORD: We will now pause for station recuperation.

That was music in a slightly different vein—I think, varicose.

There's never a dull moment on this show. Hours, yes!

This is a 5,000-watt station. I don't know what that means, but if the wind is right, they can hear us in the lobby!

I'd like to stop for a commercial. Stop for one? The way business has been, I'd even back up for one!

The problem with working in radio is, sometimes you get the feeling that nobody is listening. I'll ask my engineer. Sam, do you ever get the feeling nobody is listening? . . . Sam?

This is the "_____ Show" and I'd like to say it's the top-rated deejay show in America. Boy, would I like to say it!

DEFENSE

If we limit our defense budget any further, we'll also have to change our national anthem—from "The Star-Spangled Banner" to "I Surrender, Dear."

I have a great idea for April first. The President calls up the Kremlin and says, "I leaned on the button by mistake and six hundred atomic missiles are now on their way to Moscow. —Who do I say 'Ooops' to?"

DEFINITIONS

Busing is when you move into a ghetto so your kids can go to a good school.

A cashew is a peanut with back trouble.

Comic relief is when you add a touch of humor to an otherwise serious situation. It's like the word "obey" in the marriage ceremony.

An efficiency expert is someone who puts Murine in his grapefruit.

FAIL SAFE: What you can do when your family has money.

FIREPROOF: What you are when you have something on the boss.

LAST RITES: What you hear just before a yes-man is fired.

OVERWEIGHT: What happens when you take the butter with the sweet.

PATIENCE: What you have when your boss makes the mistake.

A realist is a husband who hears his wife say, "I'll be ready in a moment" and picks up something to read—*War and Peace*!

Recycling is a fella who sells a million dollars' worth of insurance—and then marries the beneficiary.

Speed reading is what you do when one of your fellow employees is cashing his check.

DENTIST

Did you ever get the feeling that your teeth are twenty years older than the rest of you?

I don't want to complain about my dentist but last night I went to a dinner and swallowed 1,500 calories—and this was just in fillings.

Yesterday I called up my dentist and I said, "Doc, I don't mean to be critical, but every time I eat I have to use tenderizer." He said, "Lots of people use tenderizer." I said, "In soup?"

I'm at that age where biting into a jelly apple brings me three things —memories, nostalgia, and a fifty-dollar bill from my dentist.

I often wondered how my dentist could net $200,000 a year. Then my gold inlays rusted.

My dentist really charges. Last week he put in a crown. I think it belonged to Queen Elizabeth!

Gold is now worth [USE LATEST FIGURE] an ounce. I'll tell you how I found that out. I was mugged by a dentist.

I just read an interesting piece of science fiction. It's about an orthodontist who goes bankrupt.

Today we'd like to pay tribute to Howard Cosell's dentist. The only man who has ever seen him with his mouth open and not talking.

I love to talk after getting a shot of novocaine.
It's the only time I can imitate Buddy Hackett.

DIETS

I just went on a great diet. There are only three things you can't put in your mouth—a knife, a fork, and a spoon!

Even marriage changes. Ten years ago I put my wife on a pedestal. Yesterday I put her on a diet.

The whole secret of dieting is willpower. You know what willpower is. That's going to a topless restaurant and looking at the menu!

My wife has come up with a very simple device to make me lose weight. It's called a food bill.

I don't mind telling you, I'm very discouraged. I've come to the conclusion the only way I'm going to have a young-looking body is to wear a diaper.

DIRECT MAIL

Where else but in America could you get an advertising piece that costs $50,000 to design, $500,000 to print, offers $2,000,000 in prizes —and what is it called? Junk mail!

Because of the postal increases, some American firms are going to eliminate direct mail advertising. It'll be the first time in history a postage stamp ever licked *us!*

Occupant mail can make one quite bitter;
It's 20 percent letter and 80 percent litter!

DISSENT

Remember the good old days when the only time you heard the word "dissent" was in Brooklyn post offices? "Lady, you want dis sent?"

Do you ever get the feeling that radicals have 12 million spokesmen and one listener?

I spent Sunday morning listening to a vocal minority group—the Mormon Tabernacle Choir.

There's so much anger in the world. Yesterday the tire of a used car kicked *me*.

Personally, I think all this fighting and screaming and yelling and brawling is good for kids. It prepares them for marriage.

People are so angry these days. I know a fortune-teller who no longer reads palms—fists!

DIVORCE

I feel good tonight. My wife is always trying to keep up with the neighbors. Yesterday they got a divorce.

Who knows what evil lurks in the hearts of men?
My uncle. He's a divorce lawyer.

You have to excuse me. I'm a little upset these days. I'm going through a change of wife.

They say one picture is worth ten thousand words. I found that out in divorce court. My lawyer had ten thousand words and my wife had one picture—of me and my secretary.

But I felt pretty good about getting a divorce in California because everything is community property. Then I talked to my wife—Sarah Community.

All I can say is: The man who said, "Talk is cheap"—never said, "I do."

But the biggest expense in getting a divorce isn't the lawyer's fee. It isn't even the settlement. It's editing all those home movies.

I saw a marriage break up so fast, the two figures on the wedding cake were lawyers.

They got a divorce on the morning after their wedding. It doesn't make sense. How bad could breakfast have been?

Can you imagine getting a divorce on the morning after your wedding? The biggest problem would be who gets custody of the toast!

What could happen so fast? On the morning after my wedding, I was still trying to unhook her bra!

Even their friends knew the marriage wasn't going to work out. Six of the wedding checks were postdated.

The only time I really get upset with my daughter is on the first of the month, when I write out those three checks—to the caterer, the obstetrician, and the divorce lawyer.

DOCTORS

I just got back from the doctor's. I swear, there are so many things wrong with me, I don't know whether I was made in heaven or Detroit!

I've had so many tongue depressors in my mouth, my three favorite flavors are vanilla, chocolate, and wood!

There are two things that always upset me about going to a doctor's office. When they leave the door ajar—and when they hand you one!

I've learned one thing about doctors. After an examination, a long, slow, thoughtful, confident nod means: "Your guess is as good as mine."

He's a very thorough doctor. One time I had German measles. He gave me two shots—East and West!

If you really want to bug a doctor, it's easy. When he says, "Strip to the waist!"—take off your pants!

I'm beginning to wonder about this doctor. I mean, it's all right to take out my appendix and my tonsils—but through the same incision?

My doctor said I had a trick knee. I didn't believe him until it asked me to take a card.

There are two things about my doctor that worry me. One—he writes all of his prescriptions in Latin. Two—Latin is a dead language.

Let's be honest, my doctor has made some monumental mistakes. If you want to see the monuments, they're in [LOCAL CEMETERY].

Now I lay me down to sleep,
I pray the Lord my soul to keep;
If I should die before dawn's crack,
Tell my doctor he's a no-good quack!

I'll tell you how I know this doctor is a quack. Last year I waited three months for the result of my physical and it said I had only two weeks to live!

My doctor doesn't exactly have a bedside manner.
Last night he told the president of the Excedrin Company to take two aspirin and call him in the morning.

My doctor has a peculiar sense of humor. Yesterday he fitted me for a combination neck brace, back support, and hernia belt. Said I should wear it in good health!

I once called up an internist at two o'clock in the morning and I said, "Doc, I want you to make a house call. Now get out your pad and pencil and I'll tell you where to go." You know, I didn't have to? He told me first!

It's so unusual for a doctor to make a house call, if I ever came home and found a doctor in my wife's bedroom—she'd better have her clothes off!

A husband goes into a doctor's office and says, "Doc, I want to talk to you about my wife. Sex with Sarah is like the Fourth of July!" The doctor says, "You mean it's like firecrackers and skyrockets and Roman candles all put together?" He says, "No. I mean it only happens once a year."

Either I'm getting older or doctors are getting younger. I know a brain surgeon who's so young, they don't give him rubber gloves—rubber mittens!

We have one of those very young doctors and I think he spent most of his time in medical school demonstrating. I'll tell you what I mean. My wife is in her eighth month and he still thinks it's something she ate.

I know how a pediatrician could make a fortune. All he has to do is work like a TV repairman. If something goes wrong with the kids, he takes them back to the shop!

But if you really want an experience, go to a chiropractor. You can't believe what chiropractors do to you. The pulling, the shoving, the twisting, the cracking. By the time I left I had signed one check and three confessions.

DOCTORS' FEES

Personally, I've never read the Hippocratic oath that doctors take—but I think it's against poverty.

I think one of the first things they teach kids in medical school is, "The leg bone's connected to the thigh bone; the thigh bone's connected to the hipbone; and the hipbone's connected to the wallet!"

You know what bothers me? When a doctor says he's treating you—then he sends you a bill for fifty-five dollars! . . . I don't mind getting caught with my pants down, but at least it should be for a flu shot!

I just got my doctor's bill from when I had walking pneumonia. I think he charged me by the mile!

He's the kind of doctor who has two cars. A Rolls to go to the golf course and a Volkswagen to go to IRS.

I won't say what he does with his money but he has the only rug in town that crinkles.

I have a very practical doctor. He told me I had low blood pressure. Then he gave me something to raise it—his bill.

Show me the doctor who makes house calls and I'll show you a fella who once had his Bentley disallowed by Internal Revenue.

DOGS

A dog is a great thing to have in this city. When you go out for a walk, he protects you from the muggers you would never get to see if you didn't have to take this dog out for a walk!

I'll tell you how many dogs are in this town. Where else have you ever seen a fire hydrant with a NO VACANCY sign?

Misery is having the only tree on a block with forty-two dogs.

My dog loves to eat those low-priced pet foods that are filled with grain and oats, because I use psychology. I convinced him he's a horse!

There are all kinds of dog food on the market. Some taste like the liver of a calf. Others like the breast of a chicken. We buy one that dogs can't resist. Tastes like the leg of a sofa.

We have a dog who loves to chew up furniture.
You know how some dogs have worms? He has termites!

We call him Spot. He's not a Dalmatian.
It's what he does to the rug.

The way people pamper their pets is ridiculous. Have you heard the latest? Elevator paws for dachshunds!

Did you hear about the fox terrier who won a million-dollar lottery, bought an exclusive apartment house, and wouldn't allow landlords?

Did you hear about the two dogs who were watching an X-rated movie in a drive-in theater? Finally one nudged the other and said, "How do you like that? And us they throw water on!"

DOLLAR

The dollar depreciates, by and by;
I don't complain—so do I!

I wish they wouldn't keep referring to the American dollar as stable. You know what's found in stables.

Our money has really lost its value in Europe. Yesterday a tourist threw three American coins in the fountain—and got a summons for littering.

The Europeans claim we're just grinding out printing press money. I didn't believe it until I saw the new dollar bill. It says IN GUTENBERG WE TRUST.

It's embarrassing. Last week the dollar dropped so fast, George Washington got the bends.

You've heard of the Chinese water torture? This is the American dollar torture. Those little drops can drive you crazy.

Years ago it was kids who didn't know the value of the dollar. Now it's Britain, France, Germany, and Japan.

I wish they'd stop saying the dollar needs more support. If there's one thing I can't stand it's a varicose dollar.

Did you ever figure to see the day when dollars to doughnuts was an even bet?

DRINKING

Circumstances alter cases. So do bartenders.

"America needs a return to the basic standards of morality, integrity, and honesty!" said the bartender as he rang up the price of a martini —fifteen cents.

Drinking never hurt anybody—and if you listen to the Top Forty, it helps!

My local bar has a carry-out service. You sit there for three hours and what they carry out is you.

I had a tragedy in the family this week. My drinking uncle was run over by a steamroller. Do you know what it's like being run over by a steamroller? I must say my aunt held up pretty well through the service, right up until they started to lower the envelope into the ground.

I didn't know my neighbor drank until he added a 20 percent tip to something—his income tax!

Drink? He does so much falling down, the neighbors think he's a lawn ornament.

Twenty years ago my neighbor's wife said, "Lips that touch liquor will never touch mine!" Maybe you know her. She's the one with the dusty lips!

My wife drinks and it's not her fault. It's my fault. Every time I pour her a cocktail, I tell her, "Say when!"—and she stutters.

I'll tell you how I found out my wife drinks. She had to give up Spanish dancing. Every time she put a rose between her teeth, it died.

I had a fascinating experience yesterday. I woke up with a hangover, dropped an icebag on my head, put on my shorts, staggered out to the dinette—and my wife won a double broiler for the most original way to start off a Tupperware party.

My wife is so innocent, when I go out at night she thinks I'm attending a school for portrait painters. Because every time I call her up, she hears someone saying, "Draw one and put a head on it!"

The only trouble with drinking beer is, it makes you feel like a fuel truck—round, heavy, and full of gas!

Is it true that hell serves the finest wines ever bottled? The only problem is, you have to drink them at room temperature.

You really have to know what you're doing when you buy wine. I paid eighty dollars for a case of Château Pierre le Déceptionnaire. Château Pierre le Déceptionnaire! Then I found out what that meant in English—Sneaky Pete!

Being a public speaker isn't all good food, good hotels, and good company. There are many disappointments as well. [POUR FROM A DE-

CANTER INTO A MARTINI GLASS.] Many disapointments. [HOLD UP THE GLASS.] For instance, this is water.

I have a foolproof method to overcome stage fright. You know how that great orator Demosthenes used to fill his mouth with pebbles to prepare himself for public speaking? Well, just before I came out here—I, too, filled my mouth with something. A double martini!

I don't drink much myself. I'm one of those Don Juan drinkers. Juan and I'm Don!

Speaking of drinking, did you hear about that new group called the P.T.A.A.A.? It's parents and teachers who drink for a very good reason—because they're parents and teachers.

There's another group called B.A.A.A. It's for nudists who want to stop drinking.

I love to watch the St. Patrick's Day parade. I won't say there's a lot of drinking going on, but it's the first time I ever saw a band march sideways.

Two mosquitoes were flying along and one said, "Look down there. It's Dean Martin!" The other mosquito said, "You bite him. I'm driving!"

A topless bar is where you can always find a friendly face—and nobody watching it.

DRIVING

I'll never forget the first time I tried to puzzle out a road map. I was going to Florida and I sensed something was wrong when I stopped to ask someone for directions—Nanook.

People are so trusting. They use road maps to get places the best way. The best way is usually the shortest way. The shortest way uses the least gas. Road maps come from filling stations. They make their money by selling you more gas. What makes you think those maps are accurate?

Fellas who drive with their girl friends right beside them sometimes engage in premarital wrecks.

I've only had one accident in my life. I crashed into the gate of a nudist camp. Someone came running out and said, "Why didn't you look where you were going?" I said, "I couldn't. I was too busy going where I was looking!"

Yesterday I broke down on the freeway and one of those emergency trucks charged me twenty-five dollars to pull me off. I think it was the abominable towman.

He pulled me into this garage and the first thing I saw was a big sign saying: WE OPERATE A CASH BUSINESS. And they do. They get the cash and you get the business.

She was a very tense girl. I never knew if she had a nervous tic or she was planning to make a right-hand turn.

Yesterday my son came home and said, "I have good news and bad news. The good news is I got 18 out of 20 on my driver's test." I said, "Great! Now what's the bad news?" He said, "They were pedestrians."

Now my son wants a new car. I said, "You gotta be kidding. There's one whole fender you haven't used yet!"

DRUGS

What's happened to school kids? I can remember when they played KICK THE CAN. Now it's KICK THE HABIT!

Every time I hear the name "dope peddler," I wonder if that refers to the product or the customer.

Every college campus in America is faced with a dope problem. If you don't believe it, take a look at the marks.

DRUNKS

Hi there—and you certainly are.

I know the bars close on Election Day, but aren't you stocking up a little early?

You know what I like about him? He knows just when to stop. It was March 4th, 1952.

Sir, would you mind sitting down? You've made alcoholic. Try for being anonymous.

Sir, would you mind moving back a bit? Your breath is making my eyes water.

Sir, would you mind facing the other way?
Your breath is melting my cuff links.

You know how African pygmies destroy their enemies by blowing into a poisoned dart gun? With his breath, he wouldn't need the darts.

Please! Don't serve him any more. That's like giving Murine to a peeping Tom.

Isn't he amazing? I have cassettes that take more time to get loaded.

This may be hard to believe, but I happen to know he won the 1979 American Outdoorsman of the Year Award. In 1979, he was thrown out of more doors than any other man in America!

Sir, when you leave would you mind taking the freight elevator? That's what we use for something that's loaded.

Two drunks were talking in a bar and one said, "I got all kinds of troubles. Every night my kids are out till two in the morning!" The other drunk said, "What are they doing?" The first drunk said, "Looking for me!"

A drunk was sitting in a bar looking at a *Playboy* centerfold, called over the bartender, and said, "Pardon me, but could you tell me what this is?" The bartender looked and said, "It's a girl." The drunk said, "It couldn't be. That's what I married!"

Drink? He's spent more time weaving than Burlington Mills!

I wouldn't say he's an alcoholic. He just has the same problem as the moon rocket. He can't go anywhere without a blast.

He's one of those shrewd drunks. One time I saw him finish six martinis in an hour. I said, "You must really like to drink." He said [À LA W. C. FIELDS], "Not at all, my good man. Not at all!" I said,

"Well, what do you call six martinis in an hour?" He said, "Necessity. My wife sent me out for a jar of olives and Safeway is closed!"

EARTHQUAKES

If you're in California and you feel a tremor, there are two things to remember. Number one: Run to a doorway for safety. Number two: The doorway should be in New York!

Did you hear about the world's laziest bartender?
He puts all the mixings for a whiskey sour in a cocktail shaker, goes out to _____, and waits!

_____ is a wonderful place to live.
I just wouldn't want to bake a cake there!

ECONOMICS

If you really think practice makes perfect—
watch the government manage the economy.

It's fascinating the way the Administration describes the state of the economy. As I understand it, we've reached the lowest peak in history.

Washington says the economy is turning the corner.
I'll tell you one thing—it isn't doing it on two wheels!

They say the economy is bouncing back. I have news—so are my checks!

We now have a seat-belt economy. Everybody is walking around strapped!

Do you realize how many economic advisers the President has? Talk about excess prophets!

I'm beginning to think the Administration's economic soothsayers are more inclined to soothe than to say.

You can tell the economy is improving. Two more raises and my take-home pay will equal my deductions.

The economy is really booming. You can tell.
Last week Detroit sold three more cars than it recalled.

I'm a little worried about the economy. I just got a check from the government and it said: "DO NOT FOLD, BEND, SPINDLE, MUTILATE, OR CASH."

Capitalism is like this: Forty years ago lead was added to gasoline, and the price went up. Now lead is being removed from gasoline, and the price went up.

I have two terrible worries. One worry is that we may never get back to the good old days. And the second worry is—these may be them!

EDUCATION

A school principal today is someone who tells the graduating class that they are the hope of America—while fingering his Swiss bankbook.

"PTA" means different things to different people. If you're a parent, it means Parents Threatening Action. If you're a school administrator, it means Principals Taking Aspirin.

What is happening to this world? This morning I dialed a number and said, "I'd like to talk to Bertram T. Partridge, dean of the Perfect Diction Institute." A voice said, "Thpeaking!"

Apathy is so common in America today, one school is giving a course in advanced shrugging.

ELECTIONS

Breathes there the voter, with soul so dead, who hasn't looked at the winners and softly said, "What have I done?"

Closing the bars on Election Day makes sense. It's the next day, when you read the results, that you need the drink!

Did you ever get the feeling that if they put a space on the ballot labeled NONE OF THE ABOVE—it would get 98 percent of the vote?

I have no problems with voting this year. I just listened to what the [PARTY] had to say about each other—and took them at their word.

Breathes there the man, with soul so dead, who never to himself has said, "Maybe I should have voted for Harold Stassen!"

Just before I went into the voting booth I said to myself, "Should I listen to the voice of my conscience?" Then I thought, "Naaaah! Who wants to take advice from a total stranger?"

I never knew I needed glasses until Election Day. I went into the polling place, closed the curtain, pulled the lever, and then I heard a sound I had never heard in a voting booth before—flushing!

An election year is when you rent a tuxedo for $30 and your wife buys a dress for $200, so you can go to a dinner that costs $500—to elect a two-bit politician.

I don't want to say anything about our elected officials but pigeons are attracted by crumbs—and you'll notice how many there are at City Hall.

Recycling means different things in different areas. In Washington, recycling is waste paper. In Texas, it's water. In Cook County, it's votes.

A voting machine is like a slot machine.
If you're not lucky, you can wind up with lemons.

It isn't easy being a voter. I've been stepped on so many times, I have a broadloom tie!

You have to feel sorry for the losers after a national election. Suddenly they're as prominent as the banjo part in Beethoven's Fifth.

Almost being elected is like almost beating a train to a crossing.

As one politician put it, "I was beaten fair and square and I'm gonna send my opponent a nice, warm, friendly note of congratulations. Tell me, how many *k*'s in skunk?"

One candidate was beaten so badly, they put a sign across his campaign headquarters: OPENED BY MISTAKE!

ENERGY

I'm really worried. Either we've had an exceptionally cold winter or my wife is carrying on with the oil man!

You think you're confused? Look at the electric company. They're telling us to cool it by turning off our air conditioners!

Ninety-degree weather is when electric companies and sixty-year-old bridegrooms worry about the same thing—power failure.

AFTER A POWER FAILURE: I'd like to say something about [LOCAL UTILITY]. I don't mind defrosting my refrigerator—but I'd like it to be my choice!

Do you think they're trying to tell us something? The electric company is running a contest. First prize is a gas range.

POWER MAD is what you get when the electric company tells you not to use the appliances that ten years ago they told you to buy!

We have a marvelous electric company in my hometown. Last year it grossed $4 million and netted $58. And it wouldn't have made that if it hadn't added a sideline—candles!

Last month my wife decided to save money on electricity. We didn't turn on any lights; we didn't watch TV; we didn't play the radio; we even unplugged the refrigerator. The electric bill for thirty-one days was eight cents. It would have been zero but [ELECTRIC COMPANY] kept ringing the bell to find out what was wrong!

EXECUTIVES

What a great idea for executives who drink—
Listerine-flavored whiskey!

The newest trend in management is very young executives. Companies are hiring twenty-three-year-old presidents for their youthful thinking and it works. A company treasurer went into the chief executive's office and said, "We owe $32 million, we have no operating capital, and the banks are calling in their loans. What'll we do?" And here's where the twenty-three-year-old president summoned up all of his youthful expertise. He said, "First—round up all the deposit bottles!"

I know a corporate vice-president who's so young, it's embarrassing. He was involved in a child-molesting case. What made it so embarrassing—he was the child!

FASHION

The Department of Health sent a mobile chest X-ray unit into our neighborhood—and thanks to the new fashions, we have a lot of mobile chests to X-ray.

The no-bra look is when a lot more interesting sights than the red, red robin come bob, bob, bobbin' along.

The problem with having a liberated no-bra type girl in your office is —she may work but nobody else does.

Getting used to the no-bra look takes time. Then again, who's in a hurry?

What with slit skirts and X-rated movies, there are very few things today that are "out of sight!"

You know why this trend towards nudity won't last?
Women will never be happy wearing the same outfits.

And now for our helpful, handy, homely, household tip: Girls, if you want to change your short skirts into long skirts without spending one cent on alterations, it's easy. Walk on your knees!

My wife is a little immature. I found that out when we went to our first fancy dress ball and she wore elbow-length mittens.

Have you noticed how the big trend in clothes today is leather? My wife has boots that come from a cow and I have a coat that comes from a bull. We don't take any chances. Before we open our closet door, we knock!

I can remember when you dressed up in a ridiculous-looking outfit and went to a masquerade party. Now you go to work!

I have one of those gentleman's valet stands. Last night I put my cerise tie around it, my lavender shirt, my powder-blue bell-bottoms, my shocking-pink jacket—and it crossed its legs.

FAST FOODS

One of those hamburger chains ran a suggestion contest on how to improve sales. One employee suggested they put meat in the hamburgers. Would you believe it—they gave him $155 for that suggestion? His severance pay.

Now there's a franchise for people who buy franchises and don't read the small print. It features take-out lawyers!

FAT FARMS

I went to one of those fat farms and they really work. The first day alone I was $500 lighter.

I always feel a little silly going to a fat farm. There's something about spending $500 to take off what it cost you $5,000 to put on!

You have no idea what these fat farms are like. Two hundred starving people standing around counting the minutes to the next meal. It's the first time I ever saw a waiter hijacked for his rolls!

Then they put us in the steam room and that's really something. Everybody's standing around in sheets, sweating. It's like a Ku Klux Klan meeting in Watts.

They put you on a very strict diet. It starts off with three martinis, sour cream and blintzes, roast beef and baked potatoes dripping with butter, and two slices of apple pie à la mode. They show this to you and then you have your first meal—you eat your heart out!

I lost so much weight, people kept looking at my ankles. Why not? That's where my pants were.

FATHER'S DAY

Did you ever get the feeling that the only reason we have fathers is to provide material for situation comedies?

Mom gave Dad a membership in Weight Watchers and I gave Dad a subscription to *Playboy*. I figure, let him decide whose weight he wants to watch.

Isn't that sweet? My secretary is giving me clothing for Father's Day. Tell me, what's a paternity suit?

It isn't easy to be a father these days. My daughter brings home more crumbs than a sloppy waitress!

Have you noticed how the big thing in men's toiletries is lime? Everything smells of lime and it really works. Yesterday I got a phone call and a voice said, "[YOUR NAME], ever since you started using lime after-shave lotion, lime toilet water, and lime cologne, I've fallen madly in love with you." I said, "You have? Would you mind speaking a little louder?" It said, "I can't. I'm a grapefruit!"

FISHING

Did you hear about the two killer whales who were watching a fleet of fishing boats pull in their catch? Finally, one nudged the other and said, "Look who's calling names!"

Two fish were talking and one said, "Did you hear that Charlie the Tuna called off his engagement to Minnie the Mermaid?" The second fish said, "Charlie the Tuna called off his engagement to Minnie the Mermaid? What for?" He said, "What for? Did you ever see the top half of her?"

FLORIDA

I happen to know that Florida is now working on something that could revolutionize its real estate market. It's an alligator that eats crabgrass!

There is only one problem with taking a winter vacation in Florida. You spend two weeks getting a deep, rich, golden tan—then they hand you the bill and you're pale again!

Last year I got down there and right away I put in a long-distance phone call to my travel agent. I said, "I'm paying sixty-five dollars a day and you ought to see this room!" He said, "Is it facing the ocean?" I said, "It isn't even facing the hallway!"

In all fairness, he did warn me. I asked him if you could get along in Florida on sixty-five dollars a day. He said, "If you're an alligator, yes. If you're a tourist, no!"

I should have been suspicious when he said the hotel was in North Miami Beach. North Miami Beach—that's travel agent talk for Wilmington, North Carolina.

I won't comment on the weather we had. Did you know they named a wine after the first bird who ever flew down to Florida for the winter? Cold Duck!

FLU

This is the season when you're faced with the problem: What do you say to the person who has everything—and he's breathing on you?

The flu season is when you start off in the morning with a light heart and end up in the evening with a heavy nose!

In our house the only thing that gets recycled is the flu.

If you're a husband, this time of year can be dangerous. I'll explain what I mean. What if only two people in town have the flu—you and the baby-sitter?

You know what really shakes you up during the flu season? When you tell the doctor your symptoms and he starts backing away!

FLYING

Can you imagine riding in a plane at two and a half times the speed of sound? You whisper something to the stewardess and by the time she hears it, it's too late!

Personally, I always fly first class.
You meet a better class of hijacker.

I just finished reading a book about the Wright Brothers—the two fellas who invented the airplane. Boy, just think what would be happening today if it wasn't for the Wright Brothers. They'd be showing movies on stagecoaches!

They say Orville and Wilbur Wright learned how to fly by watching the birds. It's a good thing they didn't watch rabbits! . . .
We'd all be hopping. Don't get ahead of me like that.

The last time I went to New York, it was incredible. We circled the airport for two hours. What made it so incredible, we were in a bus!

I can't help it, I'm deathly afraid of height.
When I sneeze, my wife just says, "Gesund!"

FOOD

Now here's the plan. We cross pasta with a boa constrictor. We get spaghetti that winds itself around the fork!

All this talk about food stamps. It's ridiculous. How often do you get to mail a pork chop?

My wife bought a leg of lamb last Sunday. I won't say it was tough, but I think we got the only lamb in town that went in for jogging. . . . I had to use an electric carving knife to cut it—and this was just the gravy!

There's so much deception in this world. I bought a barbecued chicken, took it home. What do you think it was?
A duck with a nose job!

Puffed rice is very popular these days. It's what you throw at weddings when the bride is expecting.

A bagel is a recruiting office for dentists.

FOOD PRICES

Prices are so high, it's ridiculous. I don't mind breaking a hundred on the golf course—but in the supermarket?

You can't imagine how high food prices are. I can remember when it was bread that was enriched. Now it's supermarkets!

Prices are so high, they used to have signs saying, "WATCH YOUR CHILDREN." Now they say, "WATCH YOUR LANGUAGE."

Prices are just ridiculous. Yesterday I went into one of those fried chicken places and spent $1.50 for a wing and a drumstick. It's the first time I ever paid an arm and a leg for an arm and a leg!

It shows you how times have changed. I can remember when people were singing: "How High the Moon?" Now it's "How High the Lamb Chops!"

Food prices are so high, last night we had a religious experience. I think it was the Last Supper.

If food prices go any higher, a status symbol is going to be a toothpick!

Food prices are so high, shoppers have the same problem as the [LOSING BASEBALL TEAM]. It's awfully hard to get the bags loaded.

FOOTBALL

You can always tell when the baseball season is over and the football season is starting. The fellas doing the shaving commercials are much bigger.

For an ideal fall vacation, why not see Effigy—a charming little town whose principal industry is burning football coaches.

Football is a game in which twenty-two big, strong, healthy fellas run around like crazy for two hours—while fifty thousand people who really need the exercise watch them!

You can't believe what some of these professionals look like. Six feet six—360 pounds. If you're out at the beach and a fella like this kicks sand in your face—do the smart thing. Help him!

Did you hear about the world's dumbest center? They had to stencil something on the seat of his pants—THIS END UP!

Fellas who sit with a six-pack in front of a TV set and watch two football games and a golf tourney bring something special into a home—divorce.

I finally discovered the reason why housewives don't like football. I was watching a game on TV and I said, "Look at that! He's sweeping around right end!" My wife said, "What's that?" I said, "Right end?" She said, "No—sweeping."

A religious liberal is someone who goes to the Notre Dame–SMU game and roots for a tie.

FRANKENSTEIN'S MONSTER

Let's all stand and sing the marching song of horror movie fans: "Gory, Gory, Hallelujah!"

Then there was the Frankenstein monster. He always walked around like this: [STIFF-LEGGED WALK WITH ARMS OUTSTRETCHED]. Worst case of arthritis I ever saw!

The Frankenstein monster never talked. He just went like this: [ROAR AND MAKE A MENACING GESTURE WITH YOUR HAND]. Fortunately I can understand that 'cause I'm married.

I'm so married, every time I see the Frankenstein monster go: [REPEAT ROAR AND GESTURE], I get up and take out the garbage.

Now they're trying something new in horror pictures. It's a Frankenstein picture with heart. The opening scene shows the monster looking up at a flash of lightning and calling, "Mother!"

Did you hear about the Martian who was standing in front of a movie theater staring at a picture of the Frankenstein monster? Finally, another Martian comes up beside him and says, "Is that all you ever think about—sex?"

FUND-RAISING

Isn't it wonderful the way politicians always try to add that warm personal touch to everything? Yesterday I got a fund-raising letter addressed: To Whom It May Concern. It said, "Dear Whom"!

As you know, this is a $1,000-a-plate dinner. I don't know who came up with that price but I think it's my dentist.

I didn't really think they were going to charge $1,000 a plate until I saw the treasurer and finance chairman wearing nylon stockings—over their heads!

Did you hear about the $1,000-a-plate political dinner that lost money? The dum-dums served meat!

The latest concept in charity is the benefit cocktail party. It gives you a chance to raise funds and hell at the same time.

This church is so prosperous, one Sunday the finance chairman took the collection—all the way to Brazil.

UNCHURCHED can mean a person who isn't affiliated with any religious organization. It can also mean a congregation that didn't think the bank would foreclose.

Most churches would have no problems if people put in the plate on Sunday as much as they take off the plate at the annual dinner.

As the minister said to his wife after counting the Sunday collection, "I just figured out why so many people are switching from drugs to religion. It's cheaper."

Many churches operate on Mickey Rooney budgets. At the end of the year they're a little short.

Let's all sing that wonderful old hymn about the church that spent $140,000 for a new building and didn't have enough left over to buy pews. It's called "Stand Up, Stand Up for Jesus!"

"My uncle's a coin collector."
"He's a numismatist?"
"No, he counts the Sunday offering."

It's called cold cash because our treasurer doesn't keep it long enough to warm it up.

I know a church that held a two-month fund-raising campaign to buy a $2,000 boiler and came up with $87. So they didn't buy the boiler. They figured they were in enough hot water already.

It's rather discouraging to belong to a church that's always asking for money. You're never sure if you're one of the flock or one of the fleeced.

I had kind of a prophetic introduction to my church's building fund campaign. The minister said, "O Lord, give us Thy succor!" And then I walked in.

True faith is dropping your last three bills into the collection plate—one from the butcher and two from the dry cleaner.

Our finance chairman didn't want to alarm you but he did ask me to say that if we don't put some money into our treasury soon, we're going to be arrested for impersonating the government.

Then there's the more direct method of fund-raising. Like the finance chairman saying, "Each member in favor of our meeting the budget this year, please raise your hand—and have a $500 check in it!"

Show me a finance chairman who believes in secret giving and I'll show you a fund-lowerer.

Even in the dead of winter, the finance committee is never chilled by cold cash.

An amateur fund-raiser says, "Give till it hurts!" So does a professional fund-raiser—only he applies a little novocaine first.

Most churches pledge their membership once a year. There's no money down and twelve months to pray.

It's amazing how many church members are like the mantis. They pray a lot but they don't pledge!

I'd like to talk to those of our members who are pledging weekly—very weakly.

We're looking for militant givers. If you want to sign a pledge card for $5,000—write on!

Be a good host to your canvasser. Invite him into your giving room.

Then there's the canvasser who reported back to his team captain and said, "I have good news and bad news. The good news is Mr. Smith gave us a bundle!" The captain said, "Mr. Smith gave us a bundle? That's great. Now what's the bad news?" The canvasser said, "He's a laundryman."

I won't say how he gets such big contributions, but his last three pledges were signed with a swizzle stick.

FUNERALS

The greatest problem in America today is procrastination. Take funerals. Why do people wait to the last minute to have them?

Have you noticed how the people who work in funeral homes all look alike? You have to nudge them to make sure they're not one of the customers.

Do you know what they're getting for funerals these days? Twenty-five hundred dollars! Now you know why they call them the *dear* departed.

I don't mind telling you, I'm worried. Yesterday I caught the bouquet at a funeral.

The reading of the will has never made much sense to me. Here's a bunch of people sitting around listening to someone who's dead say he's of sound mind and body.

Show me a fella whose uncle dies and leaves him $2 million—and I'll show you an eager bereaver.

My aunt never stopped criticizing my uncle. I can still remember his funeral service. The minister said, "Ashes to ashes." She leaned over and said, "I told you where he'd go!"

FUR

If your wife feels bad, is downright sad,
  at finding another wrinkle;
It's hard to say what will make her gay,
  but somehow I think a mink'll!

I have never won an argument with my wife. Last month I wanted to get a watchdog and she wanted to get a fur coat. She said, "I'd feel pretty silly wearing a German shepherd to the opera." Well, yesterday it happened. A burglar broke in. You don't know how silly I felt saying, "Kill!" to a mink!

I know a fella who went into a store and bought a $4,000 fur coat. He said, "It's for my wife." And his wife saw him. So it was.

Women are never satisfied. I gave my wife a brand-new mink coat for Easter and she gets mad because of one little word on the label—
SANFORIZED.

GAMBLING

The real gamblers can always tell when winter comes to Las Vegas. The chips feel colder.

OVERHEARD: "It's so discouraging. Last week Melvin bought $50,000 worth of life insurance and this morning he dropped dead! —I never win a thing."

I know a bookie who's all heart. At Little Big Horn he would have given you Custer and three points.

GARDENING

Seed catalogs are a triumph of hope over experience.
It's like having another kid.

Faith is what you find in churches, synagogues, and people who buy twenty-five-cent seed packets.

I don't know why but I've always had a lot of trouble with gardening. That space out in the backyard may look like a garden to you. To me it's more like a Forest Lawn for seeds!

Did you ever get the feeling someone was feeding your garden birth control pills?

I have so much trouble with my garden, the immortal Sir Walter Scott even mentioned it. He wrote: "Breathes there the man with soil so dead!"

The first thing you should do with a garden is turn it over. Turn it right over to someone who knows what they're doing.

The one thing every good gardener has is a green thumb. It comes from pulling twenties out of your wallet at the garden supply shop.

You've heard the expression "dirt cheap"? My garden supply store hasn't.

Scientists claim that plants have feelings and they'll grow faster if you talk to them. All right. How do you say, "Right on!" in Geranium?

For you gardeners in the audience, March is the time to plant pansies and sweet Williams—but not too close together.

They say gardening is hard work. You bet your asters it is.

I never realized how much work there was. You show me any garden, and if the flowers look like heaven—the gardener looks like the other place!

Thanks to gardening, I have calluses in places I didn't even know I had places!

I gave up gardening the day I learned that the secret of a green thumb is brown knees.

You know what I like about a garden? Every day you can have something that's fresh cut. Sometimes it's flowers. Sometimes it's fingers.

GOVERNMENT

I just heard a comment that could explain all of our problems. It went: "Of course we're having our ups and downs. What do you expect when you elect yo-yos?"

An authority is someone who knows that half the people in Washington are crooks. An expert is someone who knows which half.

No wonder the truth is in such bad shape in Washington. Look how it's been stretched.

Senators and congressmen are public servants, so we really shouldn't complain. You know how hard it is to get good help these days.

I keep having this terrible dream. That I'm part of a profit-sharing plan—and I work for the government.

I just found out why my wife and I are having such a hard time keeping up with the Joneses. They're on welfare.

The problem with welfare is, people neither love it *nor* leave it.

I know a government efficiency expert who loves to go to the ballet. Says it's the only chance he gets to see people on their toes!

Some places have a town crier. We have thousands of them. Anybody who voted for Mayor _____.

You know what this city really needs? A mayor who's on the premises as much as he's on the payroll!

In all fairness, our city government is always trying. Yesterday a plane flew over downtown and dropped 3 million leaflets. They said: A CLEANER [YOUR TOWN] IS UP TO YOU!

Graft is a thumb on the scales of justice.

Good government is when the Department of Sanitation cleans up and the Police Department doesn't.

GOVERNMENT SPENDING

The national debt is approaching a trillion dollars. Which raises an interesting question: How do you repossess a country?

This is the kind of budget that makes you wonder if the ship of state has lifeboats.

What this country needs is a taxpayers' revolt. Let's put the seat of government on Weight Watchers!

It's no wonder the government is losing money. Look at the old-fashioned way it does things. Like, when was the last time Internal Revenue ran a sale?

The Administration is really concerned about money. You can tell. Last week the First Lady gave three parties—two dinner and one Tupperware.

We may complain about government spending but it really is involved in some worthwhile projects. For instance, it just funded a $75,000 study to find out how people who don't have kids get headaches.

The Federal Reserve has increased the liquidity of money. I know it has. Mine goes like water!

I love that phrase "revenue sharing." It sounds so dignified, so important. Isn't that what a mugger does?

Revenue sharing with the government is like giving your secretary a mink coat and getting a handshake in return.

GRADUATE SCHOOL

Kids today are very independent but I notice most of them are graduating with a Ph.D. Pa's Help and Donations!

I read that thirty thousand Ph.D.s were awarded last year. Isn't that ridiculous? Where are they gonna find that many cabs to drive?

Thanks to modern, progressive, enlightened methods of education, we could be growing the first generation who ever applied to welfare in Latin.

HAIR

Women have a unique way of looking at things. For instance, if the world were coming to an end on Wednesday—on Tuesday two places would be packed: churches and beauty parlors.

I think every woman has this fantasy: that she'll come out of a beauty parlor and have to be introduced to her husband.

It's ridiculous! What do you say to a wife who insists she's a natural bluehead?

When it comes to misplaced priorities, what about women? My wife spends two hours a day teasing her hair and five minutes a week teasing me.

I'm just amazed at all the women who wear curlers in their hair—when watching the Eleven O'clock News alone would do it!

You don't know what fear is until you've shared a double bed with a wife who wears curlers in her hair! I wake up the next day and my face looks like a Band-Aid farm!

I've noticed an interesting thing about women—the more they worry, the blonder they get!

They say long hair makes you look intellectual. Not when your wife picks one off your collar!

You know when I gave up wearing long hair? The day two women followed me into a men's room!

My son has one of those haircuts that cover his eyes, ears, nose, and neck. If the barber is busy, we take him to the vet!

My kid has so much hair, three times we had to let out his beanie!

The new hairstyles always look like they were inspired by someone with two feet on the ground and one finger in a light socket.

I know a fella—his sideburns are so long and so thick and so bushy, it's embarrassing. People keep going up and whispering in his nose!

I go to one of those cut-rate barbershops. The manicurist doesn't trim your nails. She bites them!

HALLOWEEN

Pretty soon strange people wearing masks will be coming into your house, and it's known as Halloween. In my neighborhood it's known as Monday—or Tuesday—or Wednesday—or . . .

New York is probably the worst place in the country for Halloween. Kids ring the doorbell and by the time you look through the peephole, open the three locks, slide back the bolt, unhook the chain, disconnect the burglar alarm, and leash the German shepherd—it's Christmas.

The symbol of Halloween is the jack-o'-lantern—a head with nothing inside. Some of us make them and some of us vote for them.

There are all kinds of ways to scare people on Halloween. My neighbor has eight kids. If you want to scare him all you have to do is knock on his door and deliver something—pickles and ice cream.

This Halloween my eight-year-old knocked on the door and held up something that really scared me—his Christmas list.

My accountant has an interesting theory about Halloween. He said, "If you really want to scare somebody, put on a black suit, knock on the door, and say three words." I said, "Trick or treat?" He said, "Internal Revenue Service."

This year we're going to have an ecological Halloween.
We're going to fill a tub with oil and bob for water.

And Halloween is different everywhere you go. One time I spent Halloween in Texas and a little kid knocked on the door. I said, "Do you have change for a dollar?" He said, "Mister, in Texas a dollar is change!"

Have you ever taken a good look at what kids are given to eat on Halloween? There's licorice sticks, marshmallows, candy bars, apples, bubble gum, popcorn, saltwater taffy, sugar-coated peanuts, lollipops, jawbreakers, peppermint sticks, potato chips, fudge, jelly doughnuts, raisin cookies, and chocolate layer cake. All you have to do is look at it and you'll know what made Wyatt Earp!

HEALTH

You know you're overworked when you start arguing with recorded messages.

If medical science has made so much progress, why do I feel so much worse than I did twenty years ago?

When it comes to physiques, I don't have to take a back seat to anyone. Take it? I can hardly lift it!

Did you ever get the feeling on your forty-fifth birthday that your warranty is running out?

It goes back to my childhood. Even then I was weak. You've heard of support stockings? I had a support diaper!

You know you're over the hill when you don't look at *Playboy* because holding open that center page aggravates your arthritis.

I don't know if copper bracelets cure arthritis, but it's just amazing the way diamond bracelets cure ugliness.

She always gives you the impression of eternal youth and it's all because of something she puts behind her ears—tucks!

I just had my annual physical and the doctor says I'm as sound as a dollar. But he thinks I'll recover.

Girls look on me as the strong, silent type. That's because I can't talk and hold in my stomach at the same time.

I have a lot of health problems. For instance, I don't take out the garbage—bad back. I don't mow the lawn—bad back. I don't carry in the groceries—bad back. We don't even have any children—[NOD].

I sure hope Linus Pauling is right. I've been taking so much vitamin C—yesterday I broke out in grapefruit!

HEALTH FOOD

I finally figured out why they call it health food. To survive this food, you have to be in perfect health.

I met a fella I haven't seen for twenty years and I said, "How have you been?" He said, "Not so good. I have emphysema, hardening of the arteries, ulcers, bleeding gums, water on the knee, arthritis, gout, a floating kidney, and high blood pressure." I said, "That's terrible. What are you doing for a living now?" He said, "Same old thing—selling health food."

Have you ever noticed the people who go into these health food stores? They all look like comparison shoppers for Forest Lawn.

I went into one of those natural food restaurants and it was really great. Everything looks so healthy. It's the first time I ever saw a roach with a tan!

Organic restaurants are where they add nothing to the food and 50 percent to the prices.

I don't mind telling you, I'm a little suspicious of this restaurant. They claim they never use frozen food. So how come the chef wears mittens?

Do you realize what a crazy world we're living in? Everything today is artificial preservatives. Nowadays we have bread that lasts and marriages that don't.

HECKLERS

It's been such a pleasure talking to you, I'd like to invite you to spend the weekend at our summer place—if you don't mind sleeping in the cellar. One more thing—it's a houseboat.

I need you like Rip Van Winkle needed Sominex.

Sir, I'd like to leave you with one thought, but I'm not sure you have a place to put it!

Sir, about your last remark—and I hope it was.

I have an idea. Let's all get down on our knees and look for your IQ!

Tell me, would you care to step outside and say that? Good! I'll stay here and finish my talk.

I need you like Van Gogh needed stereo!

I just heard a wonderful curse: "May you be an exhibitionist and may all your victims be nearsighted!"

He says he has an open mind and I believe it. It retains nothing.

Has it ever occurred to you, you'd make a great parole officer? You never let anyone finish a sentence.

I like the way he's always smiling. I don't know if he has nothing to worry about or nothing to worry with.

Sir, I know this is an open meeting—
but that means guests, not mouths.

Having you in the audience is like getting a kidney transplant from a bedwetter!

Sir, you're a disgrace to your race—the human.

He reminds me of the flight I came in by. It's also nonstop.

Sir, how does it feel to be a beer can on the highway of life?

Sir, are you studying to be a Xerox machine? You keep repeating yourself.

I'll say one thing. When you put in your two cents' worth, you sure haven't overvalued it.

Please, let's keep this an ethyl-type meeting. No knocks!

One of the first rules in business or in life is, learn how to cut your losses. For instance, I happen to know this man is an only child.

He's the type who votes for a bond issue and then moves.

Sir, would you mind sitting down? So far you've had all the impact of a Water Pik on the Chicago Fire.

There's a man who's got it all together.
He has a loud tie and a mouth to match.

Sir, I see you've been drinking martinis on the rocks and I think they've gone to your head. Not the martinis—the rocks!

Sir, has it ever occurred to you that half of communication is listening?

Madam, you have a tongue that could slice pickles!

I like that outfit you're wearing. First time I ever saw a seersucker mink!

HIGHWAYS

Every time I take the expressway I run into the work of that great French road builder—De Tour. . . . I've veered to the right so many times I get fan letters from Bill Buckley.

You know what shakes me up? There's always a sign saying: THIS HIGHWAY IS BEING BUILT WITH $42,000,000 IN FEDERAL FUNDS, $3,000,000 IN STATE FUNDS, $800,000 IN COUNTY FUNDS, $350,000 IN CITY FUNDS—and all you can see is three fellas leaning on shovels. . . . Three fellas leaning on shovels at eight dollars an hour and another fella with a red flag at ten dollars an hour. Naturally he gets a little more. How do you lean on a red flag?

And somewhere on the sign there's the line: THIS HIGHWAY WILL BE COMPLETED BY—and the date is always six months ago. They're called bulldozer projects. The workers doze and the signs are bull.

But what really gets to me is the part that says: YOUR TAX DOLLARS AT WORK. You don't know how it chokes me up to realize that a lifetime of blood, sweat, and tears has gone into an off ramp to Bayonne, New Jersey.

Isn't that a wonderful name—leap year? Sounds like a pedestrian trying to cross Hollywood Boulevard [LOCALIZE]!

I was in a traffic jam on the Long Island Expressway [LOCALIZE] that was so bad, it's the first time I was ever passed by an abandoned car.

HISTORY

Legend has it that Columbus stepped onto the soil of the New World, dug a hole, and planted a sprig of mistletoe. Then he told the Indians to kiss their country good-bye.

Actually, for the next five hundred years the white man was very good to the Indians. We didn't give them the complete arrow, but we certainly gave them the shaft.

Did you ever get the feeling that Indians are red because they're embarrassed for us?

Historians have just discovered the original battle flag from Little Big Horn, and embroidered across it is the affectionate nickname the troops had given to General Custer: KLUTZ!

Misery is General Custer turning to his troops and saying, "Don't worry, men, reinforcements are on their way—by Amtrak!"

My son flunked history. I said, "History! When I was your age, that was my easiest subject!" He said, "Big deal. When you were my age, what had happened?"

A typical American is someone who complains about violence in the streets, violence in the schools, violence in the media—then tunes in the roller derby.

You know what's wrong with this country? We remember the Alamo; we remember the *Maine*; and we remember Pearl Harbor. When we win, we forget!

I always observe the anniversary of Pearl Harbor by doing something patriotic—like getting bombed!

HOLLYWOOD

In a way, plastic trash bags are like the movie industry. They make garbage look attractive.

I don't know what's happening to Hollywood. I watched them shoot a scene of a girl taking a bath and it was embarrassing. There was a ring around the tub—three deep!

Hollywood actresses are very grateful to the Academy Awards. It's one of the few times they get patted on the back and it's that high up!

Hollywood is now very money-conscious. If they did *Snow White and the Seven Dwarfs* today—they'd use Mickey Rooney and six mirrors.

I think that Hollywood has been amazingly tolerant through the years. Let's face it, when have you ever heard of a movie rating a church?

Hollywood is now doing an updated version of *Cinderella*. Cinderella's coach turns into a pumpkin and the very next day two people are looking for her—the Prince and Ralph Nader.

As you know, Cinderella has two stepsisters. I didn't believe they were stepsisters until I saw their measurements—22–33–44.

HOME MOVIES

I have to admit, my wife and I are sadists. We visited a couple who had just come back from Africa. They had a projector set up, the screen, forty-two cans of film—and we never asked them about their trip.

What can you really say during three hours of home movies? I'll tell you what I say—"Wow!" It's not very clever but it hides a yawn.

People really get wrapped up in home movies. He was saying, "We saw Venice and Florence and Rome and—" I said, "Our house burned down, the kids were kidnapped, and my wife has leprosy." He said, "And Munich and Hamburg and Stuttgart and . . ."

HONEYMOONS

You can always tell the brides who have a problem. They're the ones who wear a sheer black nightgown, an exciting French perfume, and rubber gloves!

One of the first things you learn on your honeymoon is, when you're carrying your bride over the threshold, always go in sideways—unless two broken ankles and a concussion turn you on.

I know a couple who were arrested on their honeymoon. He carried her over the threshold and made passionate love to her. Unfortunately, not in that order.

Talk about embarrassing moments—I know a mortician who got married, carried his bride across the threshold, dropped her onto the bed, and from force of habit crossed her hands.

A sinking feeling is what you get when you marry a shy, demure, retiring type girl; you go to Niagara Falls; you open your suitcase; she opens her suitcase—and it's full of whips!

A sadist is someone who slows down the elevators in a honeymoon hotel.

I'll never forget my honeymoon. My wife put on her sexiest negligee, snuggled up close, and in a very shy voice said, "Dear, now that we're married, can I do anything I want?" I said, "Anything you want." She said, "*Anything* I want?" I said, "*Anything* you want!" So she went to sleep.

I leaned over and whispered in her ear, "I love you terribly." She said, "I know, but we'll have the rest of our lives to work on it."

HOSPITALS

I feel good tonight. I just came from a hospital. with a great new gimmick: Bourbon tongue depressors!

Nowadays hospitals seem to have a formula. They keep you two days if you have high blood pressure and two months if you have high insurance.

And this place can really run up bills. It's the only hospital I know that takes three weeks to cure the twenty-four-hour virus.

I'll tell you how money-hungry this hospital is.
When have you ever heard of pay bedpans?

And when it comes to paying, hospitals don't kid around. I won't say what happens if you don't pay a hospital bill—but did you ever have an appendix put back in?

While I was in the hospital I met the world's most honest doctor. A nurse asked him, "What are we operating for?" He said, "Five hundred dollars." She said, "You misunderstand. What does the patient have?" He said, "Five hundred dollars."

But the doctors are so friendly. One of them kept saying, "How's every little thing?" I didn't mind that so much but he was examining my head at the time!

Now, the first thing a hospital does is give you a gown to wear—and these gowns come in three different sizes: SHORT, SHORTER, and DON'T REACH FOR THE COOKIE JAR!

Hospital gowns are like medical insurance policies. They only cover you partway. . . . In the front it's cotton and in the back it's you!

It took me time, but I think I finally figured out why these hospital gowns are so short. It's their way of pushing the private rooms!

I had a private room. Really private. None of the nurses ever found it.

Have you ever noticed how nurses who give you penicillin shots and airline stewardesses say the exact same thing? "Bring your seat to a full upright position!"

They stuck so many needles into me, I asked the nurse for a glass of water. She said, "Are you feeling faint?" I said, "No. I just want to see if I leak!"

I knew I was in trouble when they gave me a hospital gown with six things on it—handles.

I don't want to brag, but I take pain pretty well. You're looking at the only fella who ever wore a starched collar to a tennis match!

You should have seen the guy in the bed next to me. Covered with bandages from head to toe. I said, "What do you do for a living?" He said, "I'm a former window washer." I said, "When did you give it up?" He said, "Halfway down!"

They use a lot of psychology in this hospital. For instance, they never gave me a sleeping pill. The doctor told the nurse, "When he wakes up, give him an enema." I slept for thirteen days!

HOUSEHOLD APPLIANCES

Nowadays, everything in the home is run by machines. There's a machine to wash dishes; there's a machine to wash clothes; there's a machine to open cans; there's a machine to take out the garbage. I know a kid who's eight years old and he still thinks the repairman is Daddy!

And laborsaving devices have really made housework a lot easier. Why, they figure the average American housewife spends 50 percent of her time in front of something operated by electricity—the TV set!

My wife has the cleanest, whitest, brightest linens in town and it's all because she uses the same product you see in those detergent commercials—new sheets!

They just put out the world's first honest washing machine. It has three buttons: RINSE, FADE, and SHRINK!

I always thought a trash compressor was somebody who ate cotton candy.

HOUSES

Show me a man who will get in his car when the temperature is twenty below; drive to the bank through a raging blizzard; then shovel a path to the front door—and I'll show you a fella who's making the last payment on his mortgage.

You should see what our house looks like. We have garbage that leaves by itself!

People keep asking me if there's much work involved in owning a forty-year-old house. Well, on my income tax I list a hardware store as a dependent!

Today I'd like to pay tribute to the local hardware store owner—sometimes known as the Ann Landers of homeowners!

Frankly, I'm not the handiest person in the world.
You can tell that by the questions I ask—like, "How do you get blood off a saw?"

Even my wife knows I'm not handy. For my birthday she gave me a power saw with a year's supply of fingers.

A happy homeowner is one who likes to fix things around the house —martinis.

They say that owning a house gives you something to fall back on in hard times. I have news. You ever try to hock a living room?

When you own a pool, the main thing is to keep it clean. If you can't vacuum it twice a week, do the next best thing—dust!

To a homeowner, the higher-priced spread is wallpaper.

I'll tell you what our house looks like. Yesterday the garbage men picked up the living room.

They say Rome wasn't built in a day. I think this house was.

I've had to apply so many layers of plaster, one of the rooms is now a closet!

The wiring is kind of interesting. Every time the phone rings, the lights dim.

I'll tell you what our roof is like. If we find a puddle on the floor and it's raining, we don't blame the dog.

It comes with faucet-type plumbing. If you want anything to work you have to faucet!

I happen to be an armchair traveler. Every time I sit in a chair my wife starts rearranging the furniture.

My wife bought some of that inflatable furniture. Have you seen it? Looks like a contour chair for Quasimodo!

HOUSEWORK

Nowadays, all housewives have one big problem. It's called the Zoo Problem. A housewife today is expected to dress like a peacock; sing like a nightingale; act like a lovebird; and work like a horse!

Did you see where someone wants to erect a monument to the Unknown Housewife? Isn't that a great idea? A housewife is someone who spends seven days a week scrubbing the floors, shopping for food, cooking the meals, washing the dishes, watering the lawn, weeding the garden, walking the dog, and being a valet, maid, and chauffeur for the kids. But that isn't what hurts. It's when someone asks her husband, "Does your wife work?" And he says, "No!"

My wife is a fantastic housekeeper. I mean, it's all right to be clean—but who vacuums a lawn?

My wife is so fastidious, twice a week she files her nails—under N.

You should see the way she wraps the garbage. It looks so good, I don't know whether to take it out or bring it in!

You think I'm kidding? Last Christmas the garbagemen gave *her* a tip!

Spring house-cleaning time is when it's very easy for a husband to get his wife's attention. All he has to do is sit down.

INCOME TAX

All the holidays are being switched around this year except one—April Fool's Day. That'll still be on April 15th.

It's that time again. Last week three things were rated X. Two movies and a fella doing his income tax return!

April 15th is when you're haunted by the Ghost of Earnings Past.

If you want to know what it feels like to be in the top income tax bracket—put a quarter in a coffee machine that's run out of cups.

You remember the income tax. It's like a do-it-yourself mugging.

If you think nobody knows you're alive—try filing your income tax late!

Do you think it will work? My doctor just gave me a note for Internal Revenue. It says I'm allergic to taxes.

Some fellas have a picture of their wife and kids on their desk to remind them where their money goes. I have a picture of the IRS.

You have to admire the Internal Revenue Service. I didn't think anybody could make that much money and not give out Green Stamps!

April 15th is the deadline. It's called the deadline because if you don't get it on the line—you're dead!

April 15th is when the money supply gets out of hand. Out of your hand and into the government's.

I think the Internal Revenue Service deserves a lot of credit. It's brought poverty within the reach of us all!

Internal Revenue spares no one. I think its motto is: EVERY CLOD HAS A SILVER LINING.

The middle-income taxpayer is sometimes called a tool of the Establishment. Tool? He's more like the nut that holds it together.

Income tax time is when the entire country is rated X.
Eighty million Americans have to come across.

I've got nothing against the income tax. It's just that every time my ship comes in, the government unloads it.

This country has a graduated income tax.
What we really need is one that was left back!

Show me a tax cut in an election year and I'll show you an income tax seduction!

You can always tell when income tax time is here. You know that outfit that sells thirty-one different flavors of ice cream? One of them is hemlock!

They say the average taxpayer works four months out of every year for the government—which is very disturbing. I'm not even sure people who work for the government work four months out of every year for the government.

But have you noticed the way the government is trying to make taxes a fun experience? It's the first time I ever saw a Form 1040 fold out!

And the people at Internal Revenue are so polite when they ask questions. Like: "Sir, there are two items on your return that are rather interesting. One is $500 in contributions to Christian Science. The other is $800 in doctor bills."

Even the President has to file an income tax return. Can you imagine the Internal Revenue Service asking the President questions about his return? "Tell me, Mr. President, do you have any liabilities?" And he says, "Yes, I do. Congress!"

INCOME TAX PREPARATION

Fear is taking your kid to a remedial math class and the person sitting next to him is your tax accountant.

I always get an accountant to do my taxes. Through the years I've found that a Form 1040 is easier read than done.

As far as I'm concerned, all tax preparation is H.

During the tax season the Internal Revenue Service has special phone numbers. They're for people who like to hear busy signals.

Be honest now. Don't you think the government gets a little personal in its income tax forms? I mean, it throws you questions Dun wouldn't ask Bradstreet!

For those of you who are making out your income tax, remember that birth control pills are deductible—but only if they don't work.

People keep asking, "What's the difference between the short form and the long form?" Well, it's really rather simple. If you use the short form, the government gets the money. And if you use the long form, your accountant gets the money!

Tell me, does anybody still do their own taxes? Taxes are now so complicated, what the U.S.A. doesn't get, the C.P.A. does!

A lot of people have accountants do their income tax because it saves time. Sometimes twenty years!

My accountant always puts a little X where I'm supposed to sign. I think it stands for the language I use.

I was just talking to my accountant. I said, "076982." That's his pen name.

I knew I was in trouble when he had to look up the instructions to fill in one space. Where it said DATE!

INFLATION

Inflation is when last week's prices are this week's sales.

Inflation is when the tip you leave at lunch used to buy one.

Inflation is so bad, in Texas they're calling cowboys buckandahalf-aroos.

Inflation is when you live like a shopping cart. You go through life feeling pushed.

I can remember when you used to kiss your money good-bye. Now you don't even get a chance to blow in its ear.

The whole idea of the anti-inflation campaign is to put a reasonable limit on profits. It's like what a bartender does when the boss isn't there.

I think we should give this Administration the credit it deserves. It hasn't brought inflation entirely under control but it has confined it to prices and wages.

INTRODUCTIONS

Our speaker tonight was to have been a very famous Indian explorer but, I regret to say, he is now recovering from a rather serious mishap. He tried to come between two young lovers. Unfortunately, they were elephants!

INTRODUCING THE PROGRAM: In case you didn't notice it, this happens to be an all-beef dinner. The milk is from cows; the meat is from steers; and now we're going to have the bull.

INTRODUCTION FOR A MEMBER OF A FAMILY BUSINESS: As you all know, our speaker tonight started in the mailroom at [NAME OF HIS COMPANY] more than twenty years ago. And he worked in this mailroom for three months when somebody took a liking to him—his father.

JOBS

Positive thinking is when you work forty-eight hours a week in a steel mill; have a part-time job as a janitor; drive a cab on weekends; and when you write out the check to pay your income tax, you say, "Easy come. Easy go!"

Our personnel manager just showed me a really wild job application. It says: MARRIED? Four times. CHILDREN? No, grown women.

I have an uncle who's a window dresser. That's what the family calls him—a window dresser. The police call him an exhibitionist.

My brother-in-law hasn't had a job in ten years and it isn't his fault. There just isn't much demand for his line of work. He's a galley slave.

One of the happiest men I know is a Customs inspector in California. One of the customs he inspects is wife-swapping.

Americans aren't quitters and you know why?
When you're fired you get unemployment insurance!

JOGGING

America is the only country in the world where people jog ten miles a day for exercise and then take elevators up to the mezzanine.

Jogging is a perfect exercise. Thanks to jogging, for the first time in history people are dropping dead in perfect health.

You can always tell a middle-aged fella who jogs ten miles a day in the hot sun. He's the one they don't have to put makeup on at Forest Lawn!

If you want to run ten miles a day, it's easy. All you have to do is put something around the edge of your shorts—lace!

That's the thing that's always bothered me. You see all these people running around in their shorts. How do you know they're jogging? Maybe they're just chicken nudists!

You should see me in the morning. Yesterday two worms were chewing on a leaf; one of them looked up and saw me go by in my jogging shorts. He said, "Clarence, do you see what I see?" And the other worm said, "Please, not while I'm eating!"

I had to give up jogging. I won't say what I looked like—but picture a plate of Jell-O in heat!

JUDGES

The truth shall make you free—unless you're a criminal. In which case, the courts shall make you free.

It shows you how uninformed I am. Everybody's worrying about the makeup of the Supreme Court. I didn't even know they wore any.

Have you seen those long black outfits? They're embarrassing. You put one on and right away you look like a hooker at Forest Lawn!

JULY FOURTH

Happiness on the Fourth of July is parents hearing their kids are shooting up—and it's fireworks.

In spite of all the advertising, I know of only one group of people who want to have a Safe and Sane Fourth—newlyweds.

July Fourth is kind of a tradition in this country. In 1776 our leaders signed the Declaration of Independence, rang the Liberty Bell, and ever since then we've had ding-a-lings in government.

LANDLORDS

My landlord is all heart. He said he's going to do his bit to curb air pollution. This winter he won't run the furnace as often.

Our apartment is so cold, last night my wife put on the sexiest thing she has—a black lace overcoat!

Dear Mr. Landlord: I don't want to be a complainer but yesterday I mixed daiquiris and put them where they could freeze in ten minutes —the living room.

LAS VEGAS

A junket is what you fly to Las Vegas on, and when you get back, it's what the teller says you can do with your bankbook.

My neighbor just got back from Las Vegas. I said, "What did you think of the crap tables?" He said, "Beats me!"

I don't want to brag but everybody takes me for forty.
Everybody but Las Vegas. They took me for five hundred.

I just got back from Las Vegas. I'll tell you one thing: The Red Cross isn't the only one who's out for blood!

LAWNS

The motto of every homeowner who has ever had trouble with a lawn: IN SOD WE TRUST!

We have one of those push-button lawn mowers. You put your belly button up against the handle and push!

Who came up with the idea that lawns should be cut? To your neighbors you're a gardener. To God you could be a vandal.

You have no idea how expensive it is. I had the kid next door cut my lawn—fifteen dollars! I said, "Fifteen dollars to cut a lawn? What did you use—cuticle scissors?"

And you should see the job he did. Cut? It wasn't even bruised!

LAWYERS

I'll tell you how smart my lawyer is. He never graduated from law school. He was so smart, he settled out of class!

He's a wonderful lawyer. So tenacious. One of his clients was hanged but even then he didn't give up. He sued for whiplash!

My lawyer happens to be the Marquis de Sade of the legal profession. He's making a fortune out of whiplashes.

He only handles personal injury cases. To him, justice doesn't wear a blindfold—it wears a bandage!

I'm not saying he's dishonest, but he believes in taking all of his cases to the jury—one member at a time.

He works on a contingency basis. That's an old gold-mining term meaning he gets the gold and you get the shaft.

I shouldn't complain. I once had a lawyer who was so clumsy, one time he threw himself on the mercy of the court—and missed!

He was one of those relaxed lawyers. He passed the bar ten years ago and he hasn't passed one since.

Isn't it great the way you always read a legal contract before signing it and you still have no idea what it's all about? To this day, I'm always hurt when I'm not invited to the party of the first part.

A paternity suit is what happens when you leave the scene of an accident.

My lawyer is so bad, if I ever have to plead insanity, he'll be Exhibit A.

LIFE INSURANCE

I don't have to do this for a living, you know. When I was eighteen years old I invented the phrase "God Forbid!"—and ever since I've been collecting royalties from life insurance salesmen.

Did you hear about the insurance salesman who spent the afternoon in an X-rated movie? Went back to the office and wrote on his call report: "Saw two people who weren't covered."

Dumb? He'd sell a $50,000 life insurance policy to a lemming!

Watch out for the fella who's an insurance agent, an estate planner, a financial adviser, and a mutual fund salesman. Right away he outnumbers you four to one.

Two months ago he sold me a $100,000 policy and last night he said it wasn't enough. I got so mad I hit him with the biggest thing I could find—my premiums!

I don't want to brag but I have so much insurance, if I go, Hartford goes too!

LIFE-STYLES

A commune is where kids learn how to live in a participatory democracy. They have to be kids. Anybody with dentures could never say participatory.

Psychologists keep saying there is no longer any authority in the home, which is ridiculous. There is plenty of authority in the home. What my kids say, goes!

This morning I heard my wife talking to the furniture store. She said, "I have a drip in my water mattress." I said, "Dear, I don't ask for praise but I do demand respect!"

WANTED: Four weight lifters.
OBJECT: To turn my water mattress.

If you have a water mattress, the first thing you look for in a girl friend is short toenails!

Washington, D.C., is a curious blend of high tensions and high living. One of the crucial questions that has to be faced each day is: "What wine goes with aspirin?"

A folk singer is someone who sings about the joys of the simple life— using a $5,000 sound system.

A lot of people today are like acupuncture—they work, but they don't know why they work!

I know a couple—she's overweight and he's neurotic—and they're a sensation at masquerade balls. They go as a horse and buggy!

A priest getting married is nothing new. Nowadays you'd be surprised how many men are fathers on their wedding day.

With all this talk about priests getting married, have you ever considered how awkward it is the first time one of them makes his move? He asks the girl to come closer and it's like a famous hymn. She says, "Nearer? My God! To thee?"

When it comes to endangered species, how about people who say "Thank you"?

As any woman will tell you, there are three major parties in America today—Republican, Democratic, and Tupperware.

Kids are unbelievable. My daughter today is reading books on the bus that twenty years ago would have embarrassed our family doctor!

Presenting the shortest history book in the world: Many, many years ago there was a garden called Eden. In this garden there lived two people—Adam and Bruce.

I'd live within my income but it's such a poor neighborhood.

LITTLE LEAGUE

Last night I umpired my first Little League baseball game. If you've never been to one, it's like World War II with innings.

My kid is in the Little Leagues. He's the greatest pitcher this team ever had. Last week he threw the ball six times—didn't miss the bat once!

Little League is where the kid on the mound has five basic pitches—a fast ball, a slow ball, a curve, a sinker, and one that reaches the plate.

LOGIC

It doesn't make sense—like a ten-thousand-car motorcade to protest air pollution.

It doesn't make sense—like a masochist taking aspirin.

It doesn't make sense—like giving my brother-in-law work clothes.

It doesn't make sense—like jogging two miles to buy cigarettes.

It doesn't make sense—like singing "O Come All Ye Faithful" at a wife-swapping party.

MARRIAGE

People just don't take marriage seriously anymore. You can tell. There's a department store downtown that carries its wedding gowns in the sporting goods section.

I had my doubts about this marriage thirty minutes before the ceremony—when the bride and groom were flipping a coin to see who got to wear the gown.

The Three Ages of Marriage: Twenty is when you watch Johnny Carson after. Forty is when you watch Johnny Carson during. Sixty is when you watch Johnny Carson instead.

Marriage is something, it's plain to see,
That starts off X and ends up G.

Love is never having to say you're sorry. Marriage is never having a chance to say anything.

Marriage is when you see a fella in his slippers and bathrobe taking out the garbage on a cold, rainy night—and you recognize him. It's you!

They even have one of those sexy after-shave lotions called TAKE OUT THE GARBAGE. You put it on and, five minutes later, they're all over you. Not women—ants!

I just read that last year 4,153,237 people got married. I don't want to start any trouble, but shouldn't that be an even number?

I think the romance has gone out of our marriage. My wife just sent me a twenty-fifth anniversary card. It was addressed to Occupant.

We would have gotten a divorce long ago but we tried to work it out —for the sake of the home movies.

I'm so unlucky, I have a collie, a fox terrier, and a poodle—and the only one who barks at me is my wife.

My wife and I had a very interesting family fight today. She claims the car is in more of our home movies than she is.

I know a fella who wants to get married but he can't.
He's a pacifist.

My wife and I had a rather interesting fight last night. She said it was five days since our last fight—and I said it was four.

Marriage is nature's way of keeping people from fighting with strangers!

I'll tell you what our house is like. We have three priests living with us who want to get married. The church sent them over to change their mind.

Some husbands complain that their wives don't do anything when they make love. Now my wife isn't like that. She crochets. . . .
You've heard of the rhythm method?
With us it's knit one, purl two!

Men, when you get married, the first thing you should do is take your little black address book and burn it—into your memory!

My wife is always accusing me of running around with other women. What does she mean by that "running around with other women"? It's like I joined the track team at the YWCA.

Believe me, running around with women will never get you into trouble. It's the pit stops!

Fortunately, I have something that lets me see the funny side of marriage—a microscope.

I just heard an interesting conversation in the lobby. A wife was saying to her husband, "Tell me, dear. Before we got married, did you say you were oversexed or over sex?"

Kids today don't wait. I went to a wedding where the bride was given away by her father—not to mention her waistline.

They had three figures on top of the wedding cake—
the bride, the groom, and an obstetrician.

I love to read those advice columns in the newspaper. I read one this morning. It said, "What's the worst thing a wife can get on her twenty-fifth wedding anniversary?" And you know what the answer is? "Morning sickness!"

There's no question that sometimes the romance does go out of a marriage. If you've been married twenty-five years, foreplay is a nudge.

MARRIAGE COUNSELORS

One marriage counselor doesn't waste any time.
He has a sign on his door: KNOCK—THEN KNOCK IT OFF!

Did you hear about the couple who met in a marriage counselor's office for an attempt at reconciliation? The husband said, "Look, we've both said and done things we shouldn't have. Let's forget about all that and go back to the way it was on our honeymoon. We'll go home and I'll make passionate love to you!" She said, "Over my dead body." He said, "That's right. We won't change a thing!"

We should all be very grateful to our neighbors. Just think, a marriage counselor gets twenty-five dollars an hour to listen to a couple yelling and screaming and fighting. Neighbors do it for nothing.

MAYORS

Listening to the mayor talk about taxes is a preview of coming extractions.

This is the only town where if the mayor really likes you, he gives you the key out of the city!

We have a great mayor. He's the one who took crime out of the back alleys and put it right out on the street where we can keep an eye on it.

You read some of the statements coming out of City Hall and you realize not all of the ding-a-lings are on ice cream trucks.

I once visited City Hall when the mayor was making one of his critical decisions. I didn't actually see the mayor but I did see the coin being flipped.

MEDICAL INSURANCE

Major Medical has made it possible for millions of Americans to be ill at ease.

I'm a little worried about the mail order medical insurance policy I just bought. They sent me the policy and my mailman a scalpel.

My wife and I have a wonderful medical insurance policy. We get $750 if one of us gets pregnant—me!

Insurance is a lot like wearing a hospital gown.
You're never covered as much as you think you are.

MEDICINE

You have to be impressed with medical science. First it was skin transplants; then eye transplants; then heart transplants; and now the most fantastic transplant of them all! I just read where a fella gave his seat to a lady!

An internist is the emcee of the medical profession. He doesn't do anything himself. He just points to other doctors.

They say the way to a man's heart is through his stomach. I don't know who said it but I wouldn't want him to be my doctor!

They now have a copper band that eliminates headaches.
It fits right over your kid's mouth.

MIDDLE AGE

I'm at that in-between age. I'm too young for Medicare and too old for women to care!

Middle age is the time when what sits on your knee isn't girls, it's your stomach.

You know you've reached middle age when you want something bigger on your *Playboy* Calendar—the numbers.

The first time you put on bifocals you feel like a kid again. You go down stairs three at a time—sometimes on purpose.

Middle age is when couples are reaching the *Playboy* stage of their marriage. She's folding out and he's folding up!

Middle age is when, if you take the Pill before going to bed, 10 to 1 it's aspirin!

Middle age is the most wonderful part of your life. You're just halfway between adolescence and obsolescence!

Middle age is when you start having a lot of kidney problems. The spirit is willing but the flush is weak!

Middle age is when you begin to wonder who put the quicksand in the hourglass of time.

Middle age is when you're beginning to wonder if, in the pursuit of happiness, you haven't gone right past it.

Middle age is when you first begin to realize there's one more thing in this world that's biodegradable—you!

Middle age is when you can't turn the TV set off or your wife on.

I'm at that in-between age—halfway between *Playboy* and play dead.

Fortunately I'm not getting any older. The guy in the mirror is, but I'm not!

It's an eerie feeling turning fifty. Somehow I never figured to burn out before my picture tube did.

Never trust anyone who says he's thirty—and then shakes up a container of milk before pouring it.

MINISTERS

A church looking for a minister has this in mind: He must have the humility of a saint, the administrative skills of an executive, the speaking ability of a spellbinder, the counseling know-how of a psychiatrist, and the wage requirements of an elephant—he has to work for peanuts.

If a church expects its minister to cut the grass, take out the garbage, and tidy up the building before the service—what they're really looking for is a D.D. A Doctor of Demeanity.

Did you hear about the minister who felt his sermon entitled IT'S LATER THAN YOU THINK was a huge success, because people kept looking at their watches?

Happiness to a minister is someone who snores in the same key as the closing hymn.

I know a minister who paid for his seminary tuition by working for the Internal Revenue Service. He's not much on sermons but he's great on collections!

The problem with having a too liberal minister is, you have to remind him that if he keeps telling the congregation like it is, he ain't never gonna get those collections like it was.

Yesterday I was walking by a phone booth; a fella leaned out and said, "I just got seven wrong numbers in a row." I said, "Why tell me?" He said, "I'm a minister. Would you mind saying a few appropriate words?"

Did you hear about the seminary student who took out an installment loan to pay his tuition? He said, "Get me to the church on time!"

I didn't realize how far the ecumenical movement had gone until I walked past a confessional. A voice said, "Father, I'm getting married tomorrow." And the other voice said, "Mazel tov!"

MONEY

We were so poor it was embarrassing. Pigeons used to feed *us!*

Poverty is catching. You can get it from your kids.

We were poor. The people next door were poor. The whole neighborhood was poor. We had the only fortune-teller that read Kool-Aid.

Money does bring happiness. Send some and watch us smile!

Nowadays, money *can* buy happiness. What it can't buy is anything else!

Someone once said, "Money can't buy happiness. Money can't buy respect. Money can't buy love." I don't know who said it but he's got to be the world's worst shopper!

Yesterday I analyzed my paycheck. They deducted federal tax, state tax, city tax, Social Security, pension plan, medical plan, and union dues. I looked at the balance and now I know how an over-the-hill exhibitionist feels. There's nothing left to take out!

That's a little bit of an exaggeration. In fact, at this very moment I have enough money to last me the rest of my life—providing I walk across freeways.

They say some women get terribly excited when they hear four-letter words—like SALE!

I don't know why they call counterfeit bills "funny money." You get stuck with a twenty and see how much laughing you do.

I know a fella from Dallas who's so rich he doesn't wear elevator shoes. He just had Texas lowered.

A fella who worked on a Department of Sanitation truck won the million-dollar lottery; quit his job; bought a very expensive house in a very exclusive neighborhood; and nobody ever knew he used to work on a Department of Sanitation truck. Until one day his wife opened the trunk of their Cadillac—and from force of habit, he threw the garbage in.

MORALITY

Remember when they used to talk about something so simple, even a child could do it? Nowadays they mean sex.

Kids today have a different attitude about life. If you're middle-aged, you worry about ring around the collar. If you're a kid, you don't even worry about ring around the finger.

I know a church organist who has a special tune for brides who are in their eighth month: "Love in Bloom."

I read that in 1978 over 800,000 men married girls who were already pregnant. How lazy can you get?

I don't know what's happening to this world. A fella down the street is running a back-to-school sale. He's an obstetrician.

Marriage isn't what it used to be. What it used to be is required.

But it's amazing how many couples today are living without "benefit of clergy." That's an old expression meaning: "I'm not sure. You're not sure. So why blow the two bucks?"

Corrupt? This is the only town I know that goes in for fiancée-swapping!

The New Morality has really changed things. For the first time if somebody goes into the bathroom to cry—it's him!

You can always tell a straitlaced girl at an orgy. She's the one who says, "Stop that, you! Not you. You!"

What can you really say about orgies? They're like a hotbed of hot beds.

I went to an X-rated movie,
Embarrassed as can be;
I saw somebody who shouldn't have been there,
I think that it was me!

Perhaps we should examine some of our priorities. We have rugs that don't show the dirt and movies that do.

Every time I suggest we go to an adult movie, my wife starts reciting the alphabet. She says, "X? Y?"

Remember when movie stars used to wear dark glasses so they wouldn't be recognized? Now the audience wears them!

Do you realize if you ran an X-rated movie backwards, it would be a morality play?

Remember the good old days—when a skin flick was the way you got rid of a bug?

A practical censor, when examining smut,
Gets a good look before saying, "Tut! Tut!"

MOSQUITOES

You know what I particularly hate this summer? Mosquitoes! I can't stand anything that eats more meat than I do.

That's all mosquitoes eat—meat. No wonder they're always humming. I'd be happy too!

Mosquitoes have very small brains, six legs, and they breed by the thousands. That's because they have very small brains and six legs. They keep crossing the wrong ones.

My daughter's an ecologist, so we always have religious differences over mosquitoes. Religious differences. She says, "Thou shalt not kill!" And I say, "Let us spray!"

You can always tell when the mosquito season is here because people start using four-letter words—like OUCH!

There's so much prejudice in this world. As one mosquito said to another while they watched a doctor of acupuncture push in his needles: "And us they swat!"

Do you know the government has no program to control mosquitoes? I guess it's professional courtesy. They both bite the hand that feeds them.

MOTHERS

My mother only weighed ninety-eight pounds but she was a whopper. If we didn't do something the first time—whop!

My mother always used to tell me to wear clean underwear in case I got hit by a car. Remember that? In my mind, clean underwear was so associated with hospitals, I used to have a word printed across the front of all my shorts—HELP! . . . It was great for hospitals. For dates, not so good.

My mother had a thing about waxing. She claimed it saved wear and tear on the floors—and it did. You came in the front door, and by the time you stopped, you were in the backyard!

Isn't it terrible the way modern mothers worry? Years ago when a mother was introduced to her son's new girl friend, she looked at her face. Now it's her stomach.

Francis Scott Key wrote our national anthem by the light of a rocket's red glare. I don't want to start any trouble, but can you imagine if his mother was along? "Francis—you couldn't afford a bulb?"

Did I ever tell you how a den mother once cost me $5,000? It was my den she became a mother in.

We owe a lot to mothers. Why, I know a fella who became a trapeze artist because of his mother. As a kid he held on to her skirts. Then she started wearing minis!

And now, a special message for kids: May ____ is Mother's Day. Why not do something that will really make Mother enjoy her day —LEAVE!

Entomology is a fascinating science. For instance, I learned that a queen termite lays 86,400 eggs a day and on Mother's Day she cries her eyes out. Not one lousy card!

MOVIES

The Academy Award ceremony is where the winners are saying they can't begin to name all the people who have made their success possible—and all the people who have made their success possible are sitting in the audience saying, "Try! Try!"

I saw a study film that shows the actual mating of two black widow spiders—and when it's over, the female kills the male. And all you can hear are his last dying words, "Gee, Shirley—they all can't be gems!"

I'll tell you how my career in the movies ended. We were shooting *Gone With the Wind*. The scene was set in the huge ballroom of a stately old southern mansion. Musicians were playing, champagne was flowing, hundreds of dancing couples. It was costing $25,000 a minute to shoot. I came in the door; a hush fell over the ballroom as all eyes focused on me. That's when I made my last speech in the movies. I said, "Gentlemen—they have just Sumtered on Fort Fire!"

Gone With the Wind is the story of Scarlett O'Hara. She's sort of a Roquefort-type girl—deliciously rotten!

My hometown is so far out of it, this week they're showing a Charlie Chaplin movie—first run.

Talk about creative programming. Our local movie theater has coupled a Charlie Chaplin short with an X-rated movie. It gives you a choice of tramps.

I saw one of those foreign movies and they're so unrealistic. In the first scene the boy kisses the girl on her neck. Let's face it, who can aim this bad?

I saw one movie that was so sick, the theater didn't have ushers—it had nurses!

And now I'm going to give you my impression of the language in [CURRENT MOVIE]. First, I hit my thumb with a hammer.

Tell me, what has happened to the he-men you used to see in movies? Nowadays there's a whole new element in Hollywood. I could tell the minute I saw that new adventure film—*Tarzan Opens a Boutique*.

When I was a kid, people were always trying to confuse me. For instance, I went to see a Western and they told me the good guys wore white and the bad guys wore black. So the first person who comes on the screen is a minister!

I took my ten-year-old to a G-rated movie and she had a wonderful time. I think she had a wonderful time. Tell me, is "icky" good or bad?

G-rated films are making a comeback. It's a question of mind over mattress.

But have you noticed a new sensitivity, a new compassion, a greater feeling of concern on the part of the big movie companies? You can tell it by little things. Like they just hired a speech therapist for Porky Pig.

It's a wonderful picture and you'll be crazy about the score. You come out whistling the machine guns.

They say it's a family-type picture. Who's the family? The Borgias?

It's a wonderful movie. I haven't seen so many people fall down holding their stomachs since the last time my kids cooked.

You can't blame Italian-Americans for being upset. One movie cut out the word Mafia and all other ethnic labels. They just show an average American fella sitting in death row eating his last meal—spaghetti and meatballs.

MUSIC

Isn't it eerie the way they write songs about things like air pollution, overpopulation, racial strife, nuclear warfare? Somehow it just seems wrong to face the end of the world tapping our toes.

I really don't know much about jazz. To me, W. C. Handy is a nearby washroom.

It's one of those restaurants where they have quiet background music. Well, not too quiet. The first number put ripples in my soup!

I just had an interesting experience. I sent a radio station $8.95 for an album of Oldies But Goodies. Got a nude photo of Mae West!

I always have a lot of trouble singing "The Star-Spangled Banner." The only time I can reach those high notes is when I back into a doorknob.

NEIGHBORHOODS

I live in a very tough neighborhood. Very tough. Yesterday a guy held me up with a bitten-off shotgun!

This neighborhood is so tough it's incredible. Everybody in the building next door is paying for protection. What makes it so incredible, it's a police station!

We live in a very quiet neighborhood. Nothing but little old ladies sitting around knitting—guns!

The funny part of it is, I have an eighty-year-old grandmother and she feels perfectly safe thanks to three things—a positive attitude, an optimistic outlook, and a bulletproof shawl.

I'll tell you what kind of a neighborhood I live in. The Christian Science Reading Room has a bouncer.

NEWSPAPERS

Did you hear about the world's worst newspaper? It's called the House of Ill Report!

A little boy is someone who shows up once a week to collect for the daily paper he has delivered once a week.

Is this man a reporter? If he had been at the Last Supper, his biggest quote would have been: "Please pass the mustard!"

Did you see that headline this morning—MAN HIT BY TRAIN CRITICAL? Well, you can hardly blame him.

The nice part about reading a Sunday *Times* from beginning to end is—there's only three hours left till the next one.

NEW YEAR

A TOAST: May 1980 be the prosperous 1979 that 1978 was supposed to be in 1977.

My wish for 1980 is that the army of the unemployed be the U. S. Army.

Spend New Year's Eve with your loved ones. The family that blasts together lasts together.

New Year's Eve is when millions of people celebrate Goliath style. They go out and get stoned!

I know a fella who always goes to a burlesque show on New Year's Eve and he says it's fascinating. The old year doesn't pass out—it's bumped off!

New Year's Eve is when a fool and his money are soon potted!

Everybody was drinking bridge table whiskey. Three drinks and your legs fold up under you!

I'm one of those sloppy drunks. I tried to drink champagne from her shoe. It was awful. It was a sandal!

I can remember when every New Year's Eve I used to ring out the old! Ring in the new! Ding, dong! Ding, dong! Now I just tinkle a little and go home!

Maybe I'm just sentimental, but there's something about going out to a nightclub on New Year's Eve that brings tears to my eyes. The price!

One club is charging seventy-five dollars a couple and the wine flows like water—in Lake Erie!

New Year's Eve always seems to follow a pattern. Across the country, a hundred million people are watching their clocks—and fifty thousand nightclub owners are watching their bartenders!

One club owner calls his cash register The Punchbowl—'cause everybody keeps dipping into it!

And now a song dedicated to all those people who polish off two bottles of liquor at a New Year's Eve party: "You'll Never Walk Alone"!

One balloon came floating down and hit a drunk. He said, "What's that?" I said, "It's a balloon. You know what a balloon is. It's big and round and filled with hot air." He said, "That's a balloon? You know something? I just voted for one!"

Did you hear about the nudist colony that celebrated New Year's Eve at three o'clock in the morning? No one was watching the clock!

On New Year's Day, the number of people who take Alka-Seltzer is gastronomical.

New Year's Day is when government workers turn over a new loaf.

NEW YORK CITY

There's an old New York proverb that goes: "A journey of a thousand miles begins with trying to find a parking space near the theater."

Remember that wonderful old George M. Cohan song "Forty-five Minutes from Broadway"? Today, New York traffic is so bad, you know what's forty-five minutes from Broadway? Fifth Avenue!

You can't believe the traffic. This morning I sat in a cab for twenty-five minutes and the only thing that moved was the meter.

I just heard the saddest story. It's about a New York City strong man who's getting on in years but he still wants to be able to tear the telephone book in half. So he moved to Nanticoke, Pennsylvania.

I'm glad they're finally getting rid of prostitution, live sex shows, and pornographic movies in New York. I mean, what kind of an atmosphere is that for a mugger to have to work in?

I happen to know that Central Park is absolutely safe at 8 A.M., 4 P.M., and midnight. That's when the muggers change shifts.

They say Central Park is no longer dangerous but where else can you buy a balloon for your kid and it's filled with Mace?

Anyone who walks through Central Park at night has a lot going for him.

It's so sad to watch the tourists in New York. I just saw one of them standing over a sewer, trying to get a breath of fresh air.

It's hard to describe how a tourist in New York feels, but the last scene in *King Kong* comes close.

NOSTALGIA

The big thing in America today is nostalgia. Like I've got a fifteen-year-old kid who gets nostalgic. About what? Last Tuesday?

My teenager read that Lindbergh flew across the Atlantic and he really was impressed—until he found out it was in a plane.

I get nostalgic myself. I was telling my neighbor, "Every time I think about my rich uncle leaving me a million dollars in 1955, the tears roll down my face." He said, "I didn't know your uncle left you a million dollars in 1955." I said, "He didn't. That's why the tears roll down my face."

I'll never forget the first girl I ever danced with. I said, "You'll have to forgive me but I only know two steps—the fox-trot and the tango." She said, "No kidding. Which is this?"

In those days, the only time a kid had his arms around a girl was while they were dancing. Today, the only time he doesn't—is while they're dancing.

I showed my teenage son a picture of the Benny Goodman band and said, "They were the smash hit of the forties." He looked at the picture and couldn't believe it. He said, "With only one guitar?"

Remember when girls swooned over Frank Sinatra and Perry Como? Do you know those very same girls are still falling down? Every time they take off their support stockings!

If you want to feel old, watch a 1953 movie with your kids. What's nostalgia to them was prurient interest to you.

A class reunion is where you pay fifteen dollars to be reminded of the time you wet your pants.

Remember when we went to school, the first thing you got each year was a new lunch box? It was a little tin box with a vacuum bottle and a two weeks' supply of brown bananas!

Remember that? You put a nice, ripe, yellow banana in one of these lunch boxes and three hours later you didn't eat it—you drank it!

But the vacuum bottle was different. That kept everything cold—especially soup!

NUDITY

Be honest now. Don't you feel a little silly when you dress up for the theater and the actors don't?

Do you realize that King Kong was forty years ahead of his time? He was the first big star to do nude scenes!

There's so much nudity! Yesterday I went to a movie and I heard more pants than I saw!

You can always tell who the good guys are in X-rated movies. They're the ones wearing the white socks.

They're even making nude murder mysteries. The butler did it and so did the gardener, the handyman, and the cook!

I have another nomination for the best actor. The star of an X-rated movie doing the forty-third retake!

I saw one movie. I don't know how to describe it, but picture inviting newlyweds to a come-as-you-are party.

OFFICE

Too many men today are work addicts. I was telling my secretary about a fella whose wife divorced him because he kept bringing work home with him. She said, "He was a work addict?" I said, "No. A mortician."

I didn't say he was thrifty. I just said that every time there's an **office** collection, he's the first to cheap in.

Have you noticed how every time a baby is born, right away somebody takes up an office collection? I've given so much money to other people's babies, I could have had two more of my own!

Somebody is always complaining in our office. Yesterday the receptionist came up to me and said, "I want to get something off my chest." I said, "What's that?" She said, "The sales manager."

Safes are out. The newest thinking is that you should keep your money in a conspicuous place where hundreds of eyes will always be on it. We use the office clock.

In biblical times, five thousand people were fed with two fish and five loaves of bread—and it was called a miracle. Today it's called the company cafeteria.

It's like I said to the head of the company cafeteria, "Ma'am, I just had your strawberry shortcake and I think I know what it's short of —strawberries!"

The company cafeteria had an interesting-looking side dish today. I asked the girl behind the counter what it was. She said, "It's bean salad." I said, "I know. But what is it now?"

Have you noticed that no matter where you put the suggestion box— one of the first suggestions is where you can put the suggestion box?

The girls in my office don't really respect me. Yesterday I walked in and one of them said, "Cool it. Here comes the P-R-E-S-I-D-E-N-T."

We just bought a new conference table. It's eight feet wide, thirty feet long, and sleeps twenty!

In our office, we have a little wagon that comes around during the morning break and serves coffee, milk, malteds, danish, pound cake, cheese cake, and buttered bagels. It's known as the pause that refleshes.

We have a very religious office boy. He has a sign saying "GOD HELPS THOSE WHO HELP THEMSELVES." Unfortunately, it's over the petty cash box.

OIL SPILLS

You have to give the oil companies credit for trying. One of their spokesmen said, "Of course we spilled 600,000 gallons of oil in the Pacific. It's a public service. Who wants a squeaky ocean?"

I just figured out why nobody walks on the water anymore. You could slip and break your neck!

Cast your bread upon the waters and it will come back a hundredfold. Which is fine if you like oily bread.

Pollution is affecting everything. Did you hear about the ninety-seven-pound weakling who took his girl friend to the beach—and a bully kicked oil in his face?

We have one beach that's so oily, you go down to the sea in slips.

OPENINGS

I'm grateful to be invited here to speak. I'm married and what I'm usually invited to do is listen.

WHEN INTRODUCING A BIG SUBJECT: I feel like a mosquito in a nudist camp. I hardly know where to begin.

Thank you for that wonderful introduction—even if it will add three more minutes to your next confession.

Sex, tax cut, sure-fire diet, double martini, $50,000 in commissions. . . . Now that I've got your attention, I'd like to talk to you about [YOUR SUBJECT].

If you have no objections, I'm going to read this speech. Unlike my competitors, I like to know where I'm going.

Thank you for that wonderful round of applause. You don't know how applause inspires me. I can take three bows on a waiter trying to get ketchup out of a bottle.

Tonight we are gathered here together to consider one of the most pressing problems facing mankind today: What is Little Orphan Annie doing to lizards that they're always leaping?

I want to thank you for giving me that much applause before you've even heard me. It's really an act of faith. Like being voted the best dresser in a nudist camp.

Good evening, ladies and gentlemen. You'll be happy to know that when I gave this speech to my secretary to be typed, I asked her to eliminate anything that was on the dull side. So in conclusion . . .

OPTOMETRY

This fella went into an optometrist's office and said, "Doc, you gotta give me new glasses. I can't tell heads from tails!" The optometrist said, "You're a gambler?" He said, "Even worse. I'm a dentist!"

The optometrist gave her an eye test and he said, "You have twenty-twenty vision." She said, "That's ridiculous." He said, "You have twenty-twenty vision. I'll show you the test." She said, "I do not have twenty-twenty vision. I'll show you my husband!"

I had a terrible row with my optometrist today. I said, "What makes you so sure I need glasses? How do you know the world isn't fuzzy?"

You know you're nearsighted when you either have glasses on the end of your nose—or newsprint.

I can remember when I first got bifocals. It was the day after I sprayed my wife's false eyelashes with Raid.

In this time when girls dress naughty,
Wouldn't my vision be forty-forty!

OVERPOPULATION

Everything is relative. To Cain and Abel, overpopulation was four.

The population explosion is when a teenager becomes pregnant and her parents blow up.

I have only one thing to say about the population explosion. If sex isn't a fad, we're in trouble!

You read about the effects of overpopulation and it's enough to scare the pants onto anybody!

If they really want to stop couples having too many kids, show an estimate from an orthodontist, a bill from the phone company, a bathroom that's never empty! I have a daughter who spends so much time in the bathroom, if she's gone for an hour, the mirror gets worried!

In this day and age, any couple who has more than two kids is responding to a bioillogical urge.

Scientists say we're running out of space for people. I didn't believe it until I came home and there was a guy in my wife's closet.

He must have been there for quite a while because the moths ate up all his clothes.

Family planning is very important. Like if I could have planned my family, it would have been the Rockefellers.

OVERWEIGHT

Let's be diplomatic about this. I am not fat.
Let's just say I suffer from overbite.

Fat is nature's way of explaining to you why your food bill is $200 a week.

There are telltale little signs that warn you when you're gaining weight. Like, your appendix scar is now fourteen inches wide.

Have you ever seen those old paintings of Adam and Eve in the Garden of Eden? Adam is always wearing a size 44 bush and Eve always looks like she was put out of the Garden of Eden and Weight Watchers too!

This kid really must have known her way around with a knife and fork. I don't know what the snake tempted her with but I think it was Rolaids!

If your father weighs 250 pounds and your mother weighs 230 pounds and you weigh 210 pounds—you're following in their fat-steps!

It's so discouraging. Just when I convinced my son he wasn't short and fat—he got an offer to model for cello cases.

People keep asking me, "How could you marry a girl with three chins?" I tell them the truth: "Who knew she had three chins? I met her at a ski resort!"

My wife wants us to lose weight together but she's never willing to do her share. We have the only Exercycle in town with a sidecar.

My wife is a little on the clumsy side. I mean, who else do you know can ride an Exercycle and hit somebody?

If your wife eats everything in sight—hide her glasses.

My wife's a little concerned about my weight. So am I. Yesterday we had to let out the tape measure.

Our neighbor will never admit he's fat. He keeps telling people he suffers from a very rare disease—an enlarged body!

He doesn't lose weight because he's too efficient. Too efficient. He went on a two-week diet. Finished it in three days!

Can he eat? Three schools of taxidermy are studying his technique.

Fat? For Christmas I bought him a stretch couch!

PARCEL POST

The Post Office has asked me to announce that if you mail your out-of-town packages by December 1st, they'll arrive in time for Christmas. Unfortunately, it didn't say which one.

Parcel post has eight delivery zones. It also has an erogenous zone. You ask them why it takes five weeks to deliver a package and do they get excited!

Personally, I don't mind paying fifteen cents to mail a letter. To show you what a sport I am, I'd even be willing to donate five bucks to the parcel post department—so they can buy a dictionary and look up the meaning of the word "fragile."

Last December I got a Christmas package. Crushed? I thought Kate Smith had used it for a cushion!

No, I'm only kidding. The parcel post people are doing their best. In fact, yesterday I handed one of them a compliment—and he dropped it.

Do you ever get the feeling the Post Office has figured out a new way to get packages from one end of the country to the other? It's called the dropkick.

A parcel post window is a little like a bar. It's where you go to get smashed.

PARTIES

I often wondered why men gather together at parties.
Then I listened to the women.

When it comes to conversational gambits, you have to be a little careful. For instance, "Do you come here often?" is fine at a dance. At Leavenworth, not so good!

An office party is where you spend the first hour going for drinks; the next few hours going for secretaries; and the next few months going for unemployment insurance.

I don't want to brag but I used to be the life of the party. You're looking at the only man who was ever operated on for an ingrown lampshade!

It was one of those tropical fish parties. Everybody stood around and got tanked!

I went up to one girl and said, "Gentlemen prefer blondes." She said, "I'm not really a blonde." I said, "Good. I'm not really a gentleman!"

You know what I like about [YOUR NEIGHBORHOOD] parties? The girls are so shy and demure. One of them sneezed; I said, "Gesundheit!" and she said, "Your place or mine?"

If you're a secretary, office parties remind you of William Tell. One overture after another.

I'll never forget the time I was at a party where a girl jumped out of a big cake. I won't say what she looked like, but I didn't eat my slice!

I'll tell you what kind of a party it was. It was six o'clock when things started to break up. The furniture!

I'm very conservative. When I'm at a wild party where anything goes —the first thing is me.

PERSONALITIES

Isn't she something? She has a smile that would ripen bananas!

I have a very likable personality. For instance, I get "thank you" notes from muggers.

My brother-in-law isn't lazy. He just sells a highly specialized product—dietetic charcoal for potbellied stoves.

I have a very unusual uncle. He won the three-legged race at our annual picnic. What made it so unusual, he didn't have a partner!

Cheap? Some dark night if you really want to scare him, don't say, "Reach for the sky!" Say, "Reach for the check!"

Cheap? He does strange things by the light of a full moon. He reads!

Dull? His favorite song is: "My Kind of Town, Grand Junction, Colorado, Is."

Ugly? You ever see a mosquito bite somebody with its eyes shut?

I won't say how much work he does, but I understand his paychecks are gift-wrapped.

I wouldn't say he's imitative. Then again, he's the only man I know who has a hernia from lifting ideas.

He's really a dynamo, isn't he? He's the only man I know who went to the school of experience and majored in shrugging.

Conceited? Yesterday he picked up the phone, called Dial-A-Prayer, and said, "Any messages?"

He's at that dangerous age—where any girl who looks back looks good.

Have you ever watched _____ on television?
He has all the warmth of your wife's divorce lawyer.

Is this man a conservative? You ever see a rocking chair with a seat belt?

PETS

Isn't it heartrending to walk past a pet shop? To hear the whimpering; to see the nose pressed against the window; to look into the pleading soulful eyes. And this is just the owner!

We had a tragedy in our house today. It involved my ten-year-old's new pet. Up until today, when I sat in my favorite armchair I never realized it was gerbil-colored.

I have to brag about my parakeet. I really do. Last week a burglar broke into my house, tied me up, and started to ransack the place. Well, my parakeet sized up the situation; pushed open the door of his cage; quietly flew over to the telephone; pushed the receiver off the cradle; dialed police headquarters with his beak; and when they answered, he said loud and clear, "Pretty baby! Pretty baby!"

I've never had any luck with pets. I once had a turtle I had to send to obedience school.

PHILOSOPHY

The key to success is this: First load your head with ideas—then shoot!

As Moses once said, "It isn't what you know, it's who you know!"

You know why mankind is in such trouble? We've made it easier to break a commandment than a lease.

Prejudice is ignorance put to work.

I think this just about sums up the way things are: I know a fella who's been unemployed for five years now. He's a hero worshiper!

Silence is the best diet against fat lips.

And now I'd like to bring you my Thought for the Day: When your spirits are low, why not do what I do? Use a long straw!

Some people come to the end of a perfect day. Mine is more like a factory second.

Did you ever get the feeling that life is one big basketball game—and you're Mickey Rooney?

I live such a miserable life, the only time I get to say, "Ah!" is in a doctor's office!

I'm in debt; my wife nags me; my in-laws bug me; I have arthritis; I lost a fortune in the stock market; I'm unemployed. When it comes to the will to live—sometimes I wonder if wanting to see the speedometer on my car go from 99999 to 00000 is enough.

Did you ever get the feeling that life has put you on hold?

Laugh while you can. There's nothing more biodegradable than happiness!

Teamwork pays off. Look at Niagara Falls. Niagara Falls is nothing but a lot of little drips working together.

Remember the good old days, when "putting it all together" was for jigsaw puzzlers? People already came that way.

Tonight we're going to consider one of the great questions of our time: Why the people who forget to turn off their car headlights always remember to lock the doors.

In this age of turmoil and strife and impending disaster, let us be thankful for the little things. Like, can you imagine if King Kong had known karate?

I'm not an extremist but I do believe in the death penalty. How else are you going to stop people from squeezing toothpaste in the middle of the tube?

Today is the tomorrow you worried about yesterday—and not enough.

PLAYBOY

Have you seen this month's Playmate? Talk about a fantastic figure. This girl is twenty-two years old and she still hasn't seen her feet!

Every month I look at the centerfold in *Playboy* and what can I tell you? It's the first time I ever envied a staple!

I never believed in reincarnation until I read *Playboy*. Now I want to come back as a staple!

There's one problem with reading *Playboy*. Looking at all those beautiful naked girls gets monotonous. Let me tell you another thing my wife said. . . .

I don't really think of it as *Playboy*. To me it's more like the Look-of-the-Month Club.

The *Playboy* Calendar this year has some tiptop models. Any more top and they'd tip.

A husband saw a girl in *Playboy* who measures 43–25–37 and finally figured out what's wrong with his wife—she's inside out!

My idea of poise, self-assurance, savoir faire, and personal maturity is anyone who can look at the centerfold of *Playboy*—between hymns.

Actually, *Playboy* is very educational. It's taught millions of husbands to turn pages while looking bored.

PLUMBERS

To a homeowner, the Super Bowl is one that doesn't back up.

I don't know much about things like plumbing. One time we had a leaky faucet. I spent five hours trying to get it to [INHALE SHARPLY].

I called up the plumber and said, "Can you come right over? There's a one-inch leak in the basement!" He said, "That doesn't sound too serious!" I said, "A lot you know. We're in a houseboat!"

Our plumber gets thirty-five dollars a visit and our doctor gets twenty dollars a visit. There's a great moral to this. If you have anything that's stuffed up, better it's your nose than your toilet!

Do you know what it's like to pay a plumber fifteen dollars an hour? "Good morning" alone costs you thirty-five cents!

People have heard so much about what plumbers charge, they really get uptight. One woman called a plumber and as he came in the door she sang, "This is my first repair—so please be kind!"

Some women try a different approach. A plumber finished a job and the lady of the house said, "If you'd like to come upstairs, maybe we can find a different way to pay the bill." He said, "Lady, if I find one more way to pay the bill, I won't have the strength to climb the stairs!"

You have no idea what goes on. We have a plumber who's been in the business ten years and he still doesn't know a housecoat buttons all the way up!

Do you know the worst thing you can hear from a plumber? When he says, "Uh-oh!" The "uh" is fifty dollars and the "oh" is seventy-five!

We've got a plumber who really rubs it in. I mean, who wears mink overalls?

I asked one plumber, "Why is our bathroom always stopped up?" He said, "How many are in the family?" I said, "Eight." And that's when I found out our plumber is a philosopher. He said, "Friend, plumbing is like a game of poker. You can't have a full house and a straight flush at the same time!"

I called up our plumber and I addressed him by the friendly little nickname we have for him. I said, "Sir?"

I said, "Can you come right over about our plumbing?" He said, "Is it leaking?" I said, "Is it leaking? If it was a dog we'd hit it with a newspaper!"

POLICE

Some people are concerned about coddling criminals. I know I am. I just read about a tourist who had a knife stuck into him and they didn't arrest the mugger. They arrested *him!* Claimed he was carrying a concealed weapon!

The only problem we have in this city is the secret police. If there's any gambling, narcotics, or prostitution—it's a secret to them.

I always wanted to support our local police—but the bookies beat me to it.

I'll never forget the last time I was held up. I'm standing there like this [HOLD UP YOUR HANDS] when a cop comes along and says, "Is there anything wrong?" I said, "No. I'm a test pilot for underarm deodorants!"

I'll tell you how bad the crime problem is. Yesterday I rushed into a police station to report a robbery and they made me take a number.

"Police Department? This is the Seventh National Bank. We just had a very unusual robbery. The holdup man had a stocking over his head! What's so unusual about that? The girl was still in it!"

Thirty days hath September, April, June, and my nephew who didn't think the cop meant it when he said, "Move on!"

POLITICAL CAMPAIGNS

I was trying to explain to a European how our American political system works. I said, "First, a candidate throws his hat into the ring." He said, "In Spain we put the bull in the ring." I said, "Same thing."

All right, who's the wise guy who put a sign on the back of the _____ bandwagon? It says: STUDENT DRIVER.

I know a girl who joined the _____ campaign because of a psychological problem. She's afraid of crowds.

The _____ campaign folded so fast, they named a beach chair after it!

POLITICAL CANDIDATES

[CANDIDATE] has been spending a lot of time campaigning in New Hampshire. Well, they said he doesn't have enough sense to come in out of the cold.

It's official. [WINNER OF THE PRIMARY] is now President of New Hampshire.

The primaries are turning vicious. You can tell. They now have a get-well card. It's for anyone who votes for [CANDIDATE].

I've been looking at the candidates. This could be the first primary in history where everybody runs second.

_____ is doing wonders for my uncle on Wall Street. He rents out ledges.

They say that _____ has the cleanest mind in Washington. Why not? Look how often he changes it.

This is the canning season and it's going to be interesting to see if _____ is.

I just applied for the job of _____'s concession speechwriter. It's not much work, but it's steady.

A candidate got a letter saying: "Dear Senator: I believe in the principles you stand for. For these principles, I'd climb the highest mountain, I'd swim the deepest ocean, I'd fight the biggest army, I'd cross the widest desert. Long before the polls open on election day, I will be there—that is, if it doesn't rain."

One politician is really looking forward to working the New England circuit. He thinks it's Maine, New Hampshire, and Vermouth.

One politician is so hungry for publicity he carries a little card in his wallet. It says: I AM A CANDIDATE. IN CASE OF ACCIDENT, CALL A PRESS CONFERENCE.

Let's be sensible about this. I think we should add _____ to

Mount Rushmore while it's so economical. His head is already the right size.

The nice part about _____'s program is, you won't have to envy all the benefits the poor are getting. You'll be one of them.

_____ keeps promising the little man what he really needs. I don't know what that is but I think it's elevator shoes.

I'll have to stop drinking so much coffee. Yesterday I heard one of _____'s speeches clear through.

_____ isn't exactly the most dynamic candidate we've ever seen. In fact, last week his self-winding watch stopped three times.

They say _____ is a born leader. I'll keep that in mind if he runs for usher.

Someone once wrote a song about the candidates: "Strike Up the Bland"!

I'm getting a little worried about the candidate who's in a hospital with a fractured skull. He threw his hat into the ring and forgot to let go!

They say the _____ campaign is picking up steam—and you know what steam is. Hot air that's all wet.

_____ is really going after the youth vote. You can tell by that new poster. The one where he has something on his teeth—braces.

One candidate had an embarrassing experience. He went up to a house that had a front doorbell and a back doorbell and the couple inside couldn't tell one from the other. So when the candidate rang, all he could hear was a voice saying, "Which ding-a-ling is that?"

One candidate is running for President because he hears the call of the people. He's an average politician but a great ventriloquist.

Is it true they named a pizza parlor after _____'s chances—Shakey?

Is it true that last week _____ said he has as much chance of being President as the next guy—and standing next to him was Harold Stassen?

I love to hear candidates talk about how well they're doing in the polls. I'm a bluff buff.

Then there's the candidate who's so far down the polls, his biggest worry is dogs.

Did you hear about the candidate who's so concerned about air pollution, he canceled his next six speeches?

One candidate is very unhappy with his speechwriters. He says they're damning him with faint phrase.

An ecologist came up with a great idea. He wants to make the bottom of all bird cages 8½ by 11—so _____'s speeches won't be a total waste.

They're poking a lot of fun at one of the candidates but I want to tell you something. He's got more brains in his entire head than you've got in your little finger!

They say _____ grows on you. So do warts but I've never sent one to Congress.

One politician was out kissing babies and he got a wonderful lesson in how to get along in Washington. Somebody handed him the kid backwards.

One candidate is drawing such small crowds, he's beginning to whistle-stop. If anybody whistles, he stops.

One of the candidates says his campaign is picking up speed. Isn't that what happens when you're going downhill?

POLITICAL COMMENT

People keep asking me how I got to be a [POLITICAL PARTY]. It just happened. I don't blame anybody.

Doesn't it make you a little uneasy to be called a registered Democrat or a registered Republican? You don't know if they want to count you or breed you.

The Radical Left says it will work within the system. So do termites.

A politician is someone who says, "A word to the wise is sufficient." Then he gives a two-hour speech.

Did you ever get the feeling that this might be George Plimpton's week to run the country?

Do you think this means something? The last three people I said, "Go to hell" to—have wound up in Washington.

I'll vote for any politician who wouldn't be afraid to have Jack Anderson as his file clerk.

In 1980, I want to see something in City Hall that has never been there before—me!

Frankly, I think about my opponent a lot. I even thought of him today at lunch. There was a special on bigmouth bass.

I have to admit one thing. My cigarette lighter enjoys his speeches tremendously. It's windproof.

My opponent says he's nobody's fool, which is a shame. Maybe we can get somebody to adopt him.

I don't want to say anything about this fella, but it just shows you that all the party jokes aren't in *Playboy*.

My opponent is consistent. He doesn't make that many mistakes but he keeps Xeroxing the ones he does.

He stands out like a bubble in a brewery.

I don't want to raise the question of trust, but I do happen to know that, as a kid, he collected from the tooth fairy ninety-three times!

My opponent is the type of politician people want to put on a pedestal—and anywhere else you can keep an eye on him.

POLITICAL CONVENTIONS

It's really touching the way some of the delegates went to the convention in their private jets and yachts and limousines. And they really want to identify with the common man. You can tell. It's the first time I ever saw a blue denim mink.

The average delegate was a little on the older side. It's the first time I ever saw anybody take No-Doz to make it to lunch!

I always enjoy a political convention. It's where the delegates act like Lincoln and drink like Grant.

Most political conventions are like a well-run meat market. You have your choice of baloney.

I listened to all the speeches at the convention and you know what I found out? Marcel Marceau isn't the only one who can talk for thirty minutes and not say anything!

I won't say how young some of the delegates were but I know a fella who made a fortune at the convention. He had the rubber duck concession.

A lot of magazines and newspapers printed charts so you could keep your own count on the ballots, and it was really exciting. I know a honeymoon couple who spent the whole night scoring.

They keep talking about committed delegates. The way some of them are voting, maybe they ought to be.

Between speeches and demonstrations, a political convention is where they keep minutes and lose hours!

POLITICIANS

Show me a politician who wants to rise above petty politics and I'll show you a fella who has the hot air to do it!

Watching your favorite politician on TV for the first time can be a shattering experience. It's like finding out your interior decorator is color-blind.

The truth hurts. So how come you never see a politician wince?

If exercise removes fat, I can't understand why so many politicians have double chins.

A politician is someone who never met a tax he didn't hike.

_____ is trying to eliminate poverty, which is ridiculous. That's all some of us have left!

_____ says he's nobody's man. So do the polls.

POLITICS

The _____ are the Party of Change. Don't take my word for it. Ask any waiter.

The _____ Party doesn't really have a plan. It's more like an X-rated movie. You don't know what's coming off next!

The _____ don't really have a philosophy. They just seem to be against everything the opposition is for. They remind me of the farmer who was watching Robert Fulton build the first steamboat. He said, "It'll never start! It'll never start!" Then Fulton got into the *Clermont*, started the engine, steamed up the river, and the farmer yelled after him, "It'll never stop! It'll never stop!"

Politics and college football have one thing in common: They're no place for amateurs.

POLLUTION

A reincarnated Indian who first greeted the Pilgrims in 1620—looked out over the land he once knew and said, "How?"

Industrial waste is 7 million Americans unemployed!

Even business is getting into the ecological act. I just got a bill reading HELP PREVENT PAPER POLLUTION. PAY NOW AND ELIMINATE A SECOND NOTICE.

Noise pollution is a relative thing. In a city it's a jet plane taking off. In a monastery it's a pen that scratches.

Pollution makes you feel like three of the Seven Dwarfs. You start off Sneezy, you wind up Grumpy, and if you put up with it, you gotta be a little Dopey!

One of the biggest problems facing America today is industrial trash. Some of it is being dumped into our rivers—and the rest is being dumped into our stores.

POSTAL RATE INCREASES

I get so annoyed with the Post Office. Instead of boosting the price of postage, why doesn't it just use smaller stamps?

A little song dedicated to the postal increase: "Let Me Call You, Sweetheart, I Can't Afford to Write."

First-class postage will be increased _____ percent. When you start off a letter with "Dear"—you better believe it!

The increased rates will make it possible for the Post Office to use highly sophisticated electronic equipment. Instead of a $300-a-week clerk—your letters will be lost by a $20 million computer!

POST OFFICE

I keep telling the Post Office they've got to add pizzazz to their operation—like using Bourbon-flavored glue, and every third stamp is on the house!

I'll tell you how bad the mails are. I'm still getting *Collier's*!

I have a collector's item the Post Office would love to get hold of. It's a letter to the Postmaster General marked "ADDRESS UNKNOWN."

Am I wrong? I thought we had a deal with the Post Office. We were going to show a little code and they were going to show a little zip!

Two hundred years ago a letter took three days to go from Boston to New York and it was called progress. Today it's called Special Delivery.

What is happening to this world? We've got a mailman who won't make house calls!

It's very discouraging. The Russians have something that can get to any American city in thirty minutes—and our Post Office doesn't.

POVERTY

When I was a kid we lived a hand-to-mouth existence but we never said a word. And you know why? If we did, we got a hand to the mouth!

My mother used to raise us whale blubber style. If we did something wrong, she'd whale us till we blubbered!

Nowadays a social worker is a person who makes sure that the $260 a month they give a family of four to live on—isn't being spent foolishly. It's like rationing bullets at the Alamo.

We were so poor, the tooth fairy left I.O.U.s.

It must be wonderful to be worth $100 million—to read that good times are coming back and never know they left.

PRESIDENTS

Abraham Lincoln said, "You can't fool all of the people all the time." He was a great President but a lousy magician.

Two booking agents were watching President Lincoln as he finished the Gettysburg Address. One turned to the other and said, "That's the problem with Abe. Good material, good delivery, good finish—but he can't give you time!"

My parents were so impressed with President Franklin D. Roosevelt, they named my brother after him. Maybe you heard of him—President [YOUR LAST NAME].

PRISON

Did you hear about the prison that's so comfortable, it's known as the Walled-off Astoria?

It's time we stopped coddling criminals. We've had nothing but trouble since we took the electric chair out and put the windup one in!

There are more people in prison than ever before. I wonder if the police are getting better or the lawyers are getting worse?

PSYCHIATRY

Encounter groups are marvelous. They teach you how to love friends, neighbors, total strangers, even the downtrodden masses of Asia. Everybody but your mother, father, wife, and kids.

I'll say one thing for touch therapy: What a wild way to get calluses!

Then there's the behavioral scientist who taught a lion to eat only when he heard a bell. Yesterday the lion had five dinners—four steaks and an Avon lady.

People are so uptight these days, I'm writing a book called *The Nervous Gourmet*. The first recipe is southern fried fingernails.

There are only two things to do if you have a nervous breakdown. Go away for a long rest in the country—or get a job on Wall Street where it won't be noticed. [ADAPT TO YOUR INDUSTRY.]

A psychiatrist is a doctor who's compassionate for the cash in it.

This fella went to a psychiatrist and said, "Doc, you gotta help me. I'm involved in a shipboard romance." The psychiatrist said, "What's so unusual about a shipboard romance?" He said, "I'm in the Navy!"

Some psychiatrists get fifty dollars an hour. It's ridiculous.
How much can a couch cost?

The scene is a psychiatrist's office. A patient is saying, "Doc, you gotta help me. I'm thirty-eight years old and I still wet my bed." The psychiatrist said, "My good man, that is merely an acting out of a retarded ego development and a rejection of adult responsibilities. We can stop you from wetting your bed in two ways. The first is psychoanalysis, five visits a week—fifty dollars a visit." The fella said, "What's the second way?" The doctor said, "Rubber shorts—two dollars a pair!"

There are all kinds of doctors in the world. There's the general practitioner, who knows a little about a lot of things. Then there's the specialist, who knows a lot about a few things. But the smartest doctor of them all is the psychiatrist. He doesn't know anything but he gets you to tell him!

One of the greatest jobs in America today is being a psychiatrist. Fifty dollars an hour and all the loose change they can find in the couch!

Did you hear about the lion who went to a psychiatrist? He said, "Doc, I don't know how to put this—but every time I roar, I have to sit through a two-hour movie!"

A fella went to a psychiatrist and said, "Doc, I'm really worried about my wife. Yesterday she posed for a nude picture." The psychiatrist said, "Well, I wouldn't worry about that. It's probably just an expression of her interest in art. What was the nude picture for?" He said, "Her driver's license!"

My psychiatrist really believes in positive thinking. There's a sign on the inside of his door saying: DON'T GO AWAY MAD!

I go to the world's first discount psychiatrist. It's fascinating. It's the first time I ever saw a Rorschach test in pencil.

An identity crisis is when you take your three kids to get a haircut and you discover two of them aren't yours.

PUBLIC RELATIONS

A Madison Avenue executive was taking his ten-year-old daughter through the Metropolitan Museum of Art. She stopped in front of one of the paintings and said, "Who's he?" Her father said, "John the Baptist." She said, "What did he do?" He said, "PR."

If nobody knows the troubles you've seen, you have a pretty good PR man.

I know a PR man whose wife just got a divorce. His relations were more public than he thought!

My PR man just came up with an idea that could get me mentioned

382 times in the federal budget. All I have to do is change my name to "Deficit."

I've never been able to get much publicity. When I sing, "Give my regards to Broadway. Remember me to Herald Square." Herald Square says, "Who?"

QUESTIONS AND ANSWERS

Dear Mr. [YOUR NAME]: What happened when Hannibal crossed the Alps with elephants?
Dear Sir: He got mountains that never forget!

Dear Mr. [YOUR NAME]: What is the name we give people who are the victims of vicious plots?
Dear Sir: Gardeners.

Dear Doctor: Is it true that some women taking the Pill develop high blood pressure?
Dear Reader: Only the ones who get pregnant.

A young married couple asks: "How far apart should children be spaced?" I'd say about a mile and a half!

Dear Mr. [YOUR NAME]: "Can you tell me when lilac time is?" Yes. Lilac time is three o'clock in the morning. Your wife asks you where you've been and you lilac hell!

Dear Mr. [YOUR NAME]: What does a boy miss most when he gives up his free time to deliver newspapers?
Dear Sir: The front stoop.

And now we come to Question Time. What's this? [MAKE A LOUD POP.] Give up? It's a lifeguard pulling his foot out of Lake Erie.

RACETRACK

If you really want to be healthy, wealthy, and wise—never stand in front of an open window. Especially at Santa Anita!

Have you seen those signs saying: SPEED KILLS? I bet on one horse that's gonna live forever!

Slow? Halfway down the stretch he got a ticket for loitering!

I mean, it's one thing to be a little shaky—but whoever heard of a horse with training wheels?

I always bet on those horses that fall apart in the stretch. I bet on one horse that folded so badly, he came in fifth in the race and ninth in the instant replay!

This horse came in so late, he didn't have blinkers. He had head-lights!

These two fellas in front of me were talking and one said, "Did you know if you win $600 on a race, they tell the government?" His friend said, "It could be worse." The first fella said, "What could be worse than telling the government you won $600?" He said, "Telling your wife!"

The worst thing you can do is bring a wife to the racetrack. That's right. If you lose, she gets mad—and if you win, she gets half!

People who think they can beat the horses should always remember that old Italian proverb: The only difference between a champ and a chump is a *u!*

RADIO

Have you noticed how everybody today tries to give you an argument? I called up a radio repairman and said, "I'm getting static in my FM receiver." He said, "Are you sure it's static?" I said, "No. I have the only radio in town that eats celery!"

The Shadow is the one who covered himself with a cloak of invisibility. If you've never seen anyone cover themselves with a cloak of invisibility—ask your kids to mow the lawn.

There's only one trouble with owning a cloak of invisibility. If you want to get it pressed, you have to go to a dry cleaner who smokes those funny cigarettes.

And I guess you heard what happened to Flash Gordon. Somebody found out what he was flashing.

RAILROADS

I think the railroads are putting us on. Yesterday I was on a train where the engineer stopped to ask for directions.

This train was so late, I got home and my wife had remarried.

People may complain about the railroads but I never spent three hours on one circling the station.

The government is now involved with running the railroads, which is a good thing. I've never known the gravy train to be late!

The way I see it, [LOCAL RAILROAD] is either the world's slowest railroad or the world's fastest diner!

[LOCAL RAILROAD] has given a brand-new meaning to that expression "hell on wheels."

REAL ESTATE

You have to be very careful about real estate ads. They use phrases like "a maintenance-free house." A maintenance-free house. That means for the last twenty-five years there hasn't been any maintenance.

Real estate people always try to put the best light on everything. One of them talked about a Robin Hood house. I said, "What's a Robin Hood house?" He said, "It has a Little John."

I bought land down there and I must say I had a wonderful salesman. Always smiling. I didn't think anybody could have that many teeth and not be a barracuda!

They usually give you a free dinner and I won't say the sell is high-pressure, but when the waiter asks you, "One lump or two?"—he's talking about Excedrin!

I had a salesman who could have sold bagels to the PLO.

And they don't let you leave until you buy something. I recognized somebody at the next table—Amelia Earhart!

But I do have to admit my house is in a very lovely area. It's two feet from the water—in any direction.

RECESSIONS

A recession is when your credit standing feels around for a chair.

The recession has even affected gambling. Things are so quiet in Las Vegas, you can hear a fin drop.

I'll say one thing for the recession: It is bringing the generations together. Junior still won't get a haircut and now Dad can't afford to.

A recession brings out the compassion, the concern, and the deep human feelings that are within us all. For instance, I now do something with my old clothes I never did before. I wear them!

You notice they never have depressions in Russia. How can the bottom drop out of a pit?

There is no such thing as a recession if you have the right business in the right location—like a car wash in Capistrano.

A business recession is when a country is caught with its plants down.

A company that survives a recession is like a tea bag. It doesn't really know how good it is until it gets into hot water.

Isn't it amazing how even big companies are trying to economize? I just saw an $80 million ship christened with a bottle of Yoo-Hoo!

Trying to make a profit today is like being a pickpocket in a nudist camp.

I'll tell you how bad things are in business. An executive jumped out of his eightieth-floor window, and on the fortieth floor another executive was going like this: [MAKE THE HITCHHIKER SIGN].

The biggest problem facing the country today is unpaid bills—and Sams and Johns and Melvins!

I'll tell you how bad things are getting. Bankruptcy court just asked for an unlisted number

There's a real surplus of office space downtown. You can tell. It's the first time I ever saw a landlord throw tenants in!

My neighbor owns a jewelry store and even he went bankrupt. I said, "What happened?" He said, "All that glitters is not sold!"

RECYCLING

It's like I told my wife at dinner tonight, "To you, it's recycling. To me, it's hash!"

Recycling is voters turning down a school bond issue, which lowers the effectiveness of the school system, which creates lower educational standards, which results in less knowledgeable graduates who grow into uninformed adults who vote to turn down school bond issues.

Recycling is ten Avon ladies at a Tupperware party.

Mother's Day is the epitome of recycling. It's when you borrow money from Father to buy Mother *your* favorite chocolates.

RELATIVES

My mother-in-law is a suffrajet. She flies all over the country making her kids miserable.

My wife said, "Mother doesn't feel well. Don't you think she should get out of the house more?" I said, "Hers, no. Mine, yes!"

Winning $1 million in a lottery is a relative achievement. You do it, and all you hear from is relatives.

There is one sure way to have a distant relative—
lend him money.

When my relatives visit, they eat everything in sight. That's right. The only time you see them empty-handed is when they come in the door.

I'll tell you how shrewd I am. I've been married for ten years and my relatives still don't know we have a guest room.

My brother-in-law has the best antiperspirant of them all—unemployment.

My brother-in-law is not lazy. He's just a very slow reader. By the time he finishes the want ads, it's Sunday.

My brother-in-law is a self-made man. The only trouble is, he didn't put in any working parts.

Some people think my brother-in-law is lazy but he's not. He just works so fast, he's always finished.

RELIGION

Some of the new fads in religion are so wild, it's more like Christ-inanity.

Southern California is known for its avant-God religions.

I don't mind going to a church service in a drive-in theater. But when they hold the baptisms in a car wash, that's going too far!

God isn't dead. He's just trying to break Himself of going, "Tsk! Tsk! Tsk!"

The wages of sin is death—but at least there are no deductions.

Nowadays the only time people seem to get on their knees is when looking for a contact lens.

I don't believe in all this popularizing of religion. Somehow I can't ever see myself saying, "Our Dad who art in heaven."

It's amazing how many Detroit Christians there are. The closest they come to a religious experience is buying a raffle ticket for a car.

What the world really needs is one more hymn: "I Did It Thy Way."

My uncle is a holy roller. He's the one who mixes up the numbers for Bingo.

The Atheists of America have just announced they will hold their annual convention on April 27th—God willing.

I feel sorry for an atheist who needs help. How do you pray to Charles Darwin?

I just figured out what the smile on the Mona Lisa reminds me of— an atheist in Northern Ireland.

Isn't that awful? I know an atheist who's spreading a rumor about the Billy Graham TV show. He claims they're using canned reverence.

I don't know what's happening to this world. I saw a long skinny insect standing like this: [ARMS CROSSED]. I said, "Aren't you a praying mantis?" He said, "No. I'm an agnostic."

RENT

I think it's very nice of them to return to Standard Time on the day before November 1st. It gives us another hour to figure out how to raise the rent.

I just moved into a high-rise apartment. That's not the architecture. That's the rent.

Rents are now so high, for the first time in history leases are breaking tenants!

One of the nice things about paying $800 a month for an apartment is, you're able to retrieve a much better class of magazine from the garbage.

I'm not too thrilled with living in an apartment. Paying rent is like being in the U.N. It costs you a fortune and you have nothing to show for it.

RESORTS

The most important part of any summer resort is the dining room. You've never seen such eating. Every ten minutes they have to throw cold water on the cutlery to keep it from overheating.

Eat? People come away from these resorts with black and blue marks from going like this: [TAP YOUR CHEST WITH THE SIDE OF YOUR FIST].

Do you know they got the idea for acupuncture in one of these dining rooms? Twelve people were sitting around a table with forks in their hands and one of them reached out for the last piece of meat.

People eat so much at these resorts, I know a woman who was mugged for her Rolaids!

You have no idea what goes on in these places after midnight. You know how some resorts have a social director? They have a lookout!

And the girls at these resorts are so poised. I told one of them I was a writer and I was only there to get some material. She said, "Well, what you have your hand on is 100 percent nylon."

Personally, I always use the suave, sophisticated, man-of-the-world approach at summer resorts. Ask them if they want to come up to the room and measure belly buttons!

I do another Continental-type thing I saw Paul Henreid do in a Bette Davis movie. I take out a gold case, put two cigarettes in my mouth, light them, and you'd be surprised what this gets me—emphysema!

Fellas, when going to a summer resort, be careful. In the pantry of every single girl's heart—there's a box of wedding cake mix!

RESTAURANTS

I don't like to go to a very good restaurant. It does something to me to use a napkin that has better material than my suit.

This restaurant is so exclusive, if you want water, they ask you, "What year?"

And they were having a big problem in the kitchen. The owner was saying to a new employee, "Wash those dishes!" The fella said, "But sir, I'm a college graduate." The owner said, "You are? All right, I'll show you how."

I was telling my neighbor, "When you go to a restaurant, if you really want to look important, have the busboy, the waiter, and the maître d' escort you right out to the street." He said, "How do you get them to do that?" I said, "Don't tip!"

The big problem in restaurants is tipping. Tipping is like prunes. You always have to ask yourself, "Is one enough? Is five too many?"

Do you know that I just bought my wife a dinner that cost $175—because the soup had something very special in it? Her contact lens!

They feature soup like Mother used to make—just before they took Dad to the hospital.

It's one of those restaurants where the waitresses have their hair in a bun—and it's usually the one on your plate.

You can't trust some of these restaurants. I paid $5.95 for speckled trout. What do you think I got? A herring with the measles!

Personally, I make it a point never to say grace before a Hungarian dinner. I feel there's something cynical about saying, "We thank Thee for what we are about to receive," when what we are about to receive is heartburn!

Where else but in America can you see a sign saying "NO BARE FEET" in a topless restaurant?

RETIREMENT

I'm a little depressed today. I've been paying into a plan that allows me to retire at fifty-five on twelve hundred a month. I just found out that means calories.

Retirement is when you settle back and see which gets collected first —pensions, annuities, Social Security, or you.

Pension plans are when all your life you do without steak so that at age sixty-five you'll have something to sink your teeth into. A glass of water.

Retirement is all in the way you approach it. An interviewer went up to three senior citizens sitting on a park bench in St. Petersburg and asked the first one, "What do you do all day?" He said, "Nothing." Then he asked the second senior citizen, "And what do you do all day?" He also said, "Nothing." Finally he asked the third senior citizen, "What do you do all day?" And he answered, "Are you kidding? What do *I* do all day? In this glorious land of sunshine, contentment, natural beauty, clean air, and unlimited opportunity—what do I do all day? Is that what you're asking?" The interviewer said, "Yes." He said, "I help them!"

But have you noticed that retired couples have reached a level of maturity where they never have any of those piddling little quarrels that other people do? They have one big argument that starts at seven in the morning and goes right through till bedtime. . . . Retirement is when the husband comes up with all kinds of theories on how to do the cooking, housework, and shopping better. And retirement is also when his wife comes up with a theory—that all pills don't come in bottles!

"My husband's under my feet all day long."
"He's retired?"
"No. He's a midget!"

I'll tell you one thing. Retirement communities aren't like they used to be. Remember when everybody just sat around listening to their lips chap?

No more. Last week I read about a retirement community that was raided. Caught 'em playing strip shuffleboard!

Have you ever been to one of those swingin' retirement communities? It's really something. First time I ever saw anybody mainline Geritol!

ROCK MUSIC

Rock isn't dead. It always smelled like that.

I'm fascinated by these rock groups that have all the electrical equipment on the stage. I know one musician who doubles. He plays first guitar and second fuse box.

People wonder how rock groups can afford all those expensive microphones and amplifiers and tuners and instruments. Then again, look how much money they must save on music lessons.

I wish they wouldn't hold any more rock concerts in this town. Every time they plug in the organ, the three guitars, the sixteen spotlights, and the thirty-four amplifiers—my refrigerator defrosts.

And the sound level! Have you ever heard three guitars being fed into thirty-four amplifiers putting out 28,000 watts? Sounded like Ethel Merman with her finger caught in a wringer.

The reason guitars are so popular is, they're easy to learn. For instance, my kid knows two chords. One is C major—and the other isn't.

Show me an adult who can smile through a rock and roll concert, and I'll show you a hearing aid with weak batteries!

What is so rare as a day in June?
A rock and roll hit that sounds like a tune!

That group reminds me of something. My car needs a tune-up too!

I think we should all be tolerant of rock groups. If you bent over in pants that tight, you'd howl too!

It's like I keep telling my daughter, "I have nothing against the [ROCK GROUP], but every third number, they couldn't play a polka?"

I can understand why so many kids are becoming composers. Nowadays if you have half a mind to write a hit song—that's all you need.

It's just amazing how young some of these rock singers are. I asked one for his autograph and he signed it in crayon.

It's just amazing how little spare time teenagers have—what with school, homework, baby-sitting, and explaining the names of rock groups to their parents.

Times have changed. In the forties, you shook hands with a singing star and you were so proud you didn't wash your hand for weeks. Now you shake with a singing star and *they* haven't washed their hands for weeks!

I went up to one rock group and I said, "You fellas really have good voices. You could be a great barbershop quartet!" They said, "What's that?" I said, "Quartet?" They said, "No. Barbershop."

RUSSIA

Russia is where freedom is everybody's job and you've never seen so many people unemployed!

Don't tell me what a great country Russia is until its people are allowed to leave. Freeing is believing!

There is no street crime in Russia. This is the only country where you only worry about getting mugged *after* you get to the police station.

Russia is a country of many religious convictions—
anywhere from five years to life.

Everybody is surprised at how quiet the Russian supersonic plane is. A reporter asked the Russians, "How do you keep the engines so quiet?" He said, "It's easy. Inspired engineering, meticulous workmanship, unbelievable technology, and we remind them they have relatives back at the factory!"

The big thing in Russia today is chain letters. That's right. You get a letter from the government and the next thing you know, you're in chains.

In Russia, it's not how you play the game—it's whether you win or lose. Two Russians were talking and it went something like this: "Did you hear about Krupnik? He died after losing the World Tiddlywink Championship." "Krupnick died after losing the World Tiddlywink Championship? When?" "He starts tomorrow."

I know one manufacturer who isn't the least bit worried about competition from Russia and China. He makes voting machines.

I happen to know that Russian airliners have wider seats than we do —only they're on the stewardesses.

These Russian fur hats are ridiculous. Three times last week I put the cat on my head and walked out.

SALES MEETINGS

Ladies and gentlemen, the purpose of this meeting is to hold a close order march. If we don't get some orders by March, we're going to close!

I'd like to start off this sales meeting by saying we had one of the greatest years in history. Boy, would I like to!

This sales meeting will now come to order—to see if we can get our customers to do likewise.

What our selling needs is some imagination! You remember imagination. It's what you put in your expense accounts.

For the last three weeks the only thing I've seen on order pads is dust.

One day our telephone operator fainted and it was six hours before anybody noticed it.

Then there's the sales manager who doesn't kid around. He said, "Ladies and gentlemen, the purpose of this sales meeting is to fire you with enthusiasm. If it doesn't work, I'm going to fire you—with enthusiasm."

I didn't do much over the holiday. I read some light fiction—last week's expense accounts.

SCHOOL

And now, a special message for all you parents in the audience:
School has begun,
You're feeling alone;
But you haven't lost kids,
What you've gained is a phone!

September is when millions of bright, shining, happy, laughing faces turn toward school. They belong to mothers.

Kids have gone from school to summer camp and now back to school again. It's mankind's way of recycling headaches.

My neighbor took her kids to school on opening day and the principal asked her how old they were. She said, "These two are six. These two are eight. And these two are ten." The principal said, "That's amazing. Do you get two every time?" She said, "No. Sometimes we don't get any."

I'm suffering from a low-grade infection. Every time I see my son's report card, I get sick!

I'm not sure what my kid is taking in school but I think it's an acadumbic schedule.

Nowadays there's no such thing as a kid getting left back. Mark my words, ten years from now the dumbest kid on the block will come home and say, "I just got a fud." His parents will ask, "What's a fud?" He'll say, "I dunno. It just says fud—Ph.D."

Not that I was such a great scholar. You're looking at the only kid who ever had to take remedial sandpile!

I couldn't help it if I didn't do well in school. My teacher was always saying, "Look, stupid"—and I did.

I was kind of a backward kid in school. For five years I did nothing but ride a bicycle. So they gave me a guitar to change my interest, but it didn't work. I kept falling off!

I was always getting into trouble in school and it wasn't my fault. One time I raised my hand and said, "Can I go to the bathroom?" The teacher said, "Did I hear you say 'can'?" I said, "No. I said 'bathroom.'"

When we were in the third grade, we had two big problems. The first problem was, we had to raise our hand if we wanted to leave the room. The second problem was, the teacher was nearsighted. . . . I stood on one leg so much, I got fan mail from storks!

We may have been poor, but when I went to school, I always had a hot lunch. I stole a sandwich from another kid!

Do you know that kindergartens are now holding proms? I didn't believe it myself until I saw that combination dinner jacket/diaper.

A group of teachers threatened to strike if something isn't done about violence in the schools. Don't pay any attention to them. They're just punch-drunk!

I'll never forget the immortal words of my saintly white-haired old teacher who said, "Show me a boy who talks and fights and carries on—and I'll show you a pain in the class!"

Yesterday I went to our local public school to see a familiar little figure with snow-white hair—my son. He's the one who cleans the blackboard erasers.

An interesting thing happened in my son's school today. The teacher said, "An effigy is a dummy." One kid said, "I didn't know that. You mean to say that in November, my father voted for an effigy?"

SCHOOL BUSES

So many kids are riding buses, they say a special prayer each night: "Now I lay me down to sleep;
I pray the Lord my soul to keep.
If I should die please don't delay;
Call my school and the A.A.A."

One kid has spent so much time on buses he's graduating magna cum nauseous!

It's a very simple idea. Busing is when 20 million school kids and 60 million taxpayers get taken for a ride.

Thanks to school busing, the seat of learning is now black and blue!

Busing is very educational. It's already taught two thousand drivers to stay single.

I just saw forty-five typical kids waiting on a corner. Now I know why school buses are yellow. I'd be a little chicken myself.

The way kids dress today, it's kinda dangerous putting them out on the curb at seven o'clock in the morning. One kid was picked up three times for school and twice for garbage.

Happiness is a fella who has just found out the school bus stops right next door to his place of business—and he's a midget!

SECRETARIES

You can always tell what your secretary thinks of your speech by the kind of pad she takes it down on—steno or Five Day Deodorant.

I just figured out why there are so many problems in the business world: Any woman smart enough to be a secretary—is too smart to be a secretary!

My secretary is a very literal person. Yesterday I was dictating a letter, and for the date, I looked at my *Playboy* Calendar. She put down, "January Wow!, 1980"!

My secretary always gets upset with me. She says that my heart's in the right place—but my hand isn't.

My secretary claims I'm one of the most important men she knows. Unfortunately, she keeps leaving out the *r*.

I have a very honest secretary. This morning she told a bill collector, "Yes, Mr. [YOUR NAME] is expecting you. He's out!"

I don't know how, but I have the only secretary who can make four carbons and no original.

SELLING

Salesmanship is the fine art of getting your customers to pass the buck.

Selling is a lot like water skiing. If you don't keep moving, you're sunk!

A good salesman is someone who has found a cure for the common cold shoulder.

A good salesman should never overlook the proper use of flattery. You go from show and tell to snow and sell!

I just met the world's greatest salesman. He rang our bell and I said I couldn't buy anything because I already had a hard enough time keeping track of all my bills. So he sold me a four-drawer file.

Is this man a salesman? He could have convinced the captain of the *Titanic* that it was a submarine.

A real salesman is someone who can convince his wife that the X in a movie's rating stands for Xceptional.

A sales manager has two objectives: to make sure today's sales are better than yesterday's—and worse than tomorrow's.

Then there's the proud sales manager who looked at his .map and said, "We now have pinheads in every state of the Union!"

It's one of those companies that use subtle psychological motivational techniques. They tell their salesmen to sell like all get out, 'cause if they don't, that's what they can do.

SALES CURVE: a 38–22–36 Avon lady.

I think I may have figured out what's wrong with our business. I overheard the switchboard operator saying, "The sales department is on its coffee break. They'll call you back in an hour."

Our sales department has the same problem as the Olympic rowing team. The minute they sit down they start going backwards.

Beware of the salesman who buys shoes by the pair and pants by the dozen.

Do you ever get the feeling that your sales staff couldn't sell pickles in a maternity ward?

We had one salesman who couldn't sell Blue Cross to Humpty Dumpty!

He's the sort of salesman who doesn't need leads. People keep telling him where to go.

He's one of those David and Goliath type salesmen. He's either stoned or slinging it.

I'm not saying Charlie is a dud. But whenever we get a response to one of our ads that say "NO SALESMAN WILL CALL"—we send Charlie.

SENIOR CITIZENS

"My uncle has a terrible problem with liver spots on his hands."
"He's a senior citizen?" "No. He's a sloppy eater."

Have you ever gone to a cocktail party in Sun City? It's the first time
I ever saw a martini served with a prune.

Did you hear about the two old-timers who were sitting in a Playboy
Club? Finally one of them nudged the other and said, "Did you ever
get the feeling they're transplanting the wrong things?"

I asked one old-timer, "Do you still go out with girls?" He said, "Are
you kidding? Last Friday I took the fastest girl in town up to Lovers'
Lane. We parked and fifteen minutes later she walked home!" I said,
"No fooling." He said, "That's why she walked home!"

SEX BOOKS

Isn't it amazing the ads for sex books you get in the mail? I can
remember when you took out the garbage. Now you bring it in!

Have you seen some of these sex manuals? They're ridiculous. How
do you explain to a hotel clerk why you're carrying two suitcases and
a trapeze?

I'm so naïve about things like sex manuals, the first time I heard the
word "foreplay" I thought they meant bridge.

SEX EDUCATION

Nowadays schools have more sophisticated courses than we had. For
instance, they have logic, the art of putting two and two together.
Then they have sex education, the art of putting one and one together.

You know what's embarrassing? A sign saying "EXPERIENCE IS THE
BEST TEACHER" in a sex education class.

Schools today aren't practical. We have the only educational system in the world that teaches kids what to do in bed but not how to make them.

The trouble with sex education is, some kids are getting the answers three years before they come up with the questions.

When it comes to sex education, kids today have a problem. They don't know whether to pass it and please their teacher—or fail it and please their parents!

Times have changed. Years ago you told kids the facts of life to try to convince them that sex wasn't all that bad. Now you try to convince them that sex isn't all that good.

Kids today say that sex is a sublime, inspiring, uplifting, almost religious experience, which can only mean one thing—they're doing it all wrong.

Frankly, I'm getting a little worried about my son's school. They charge $25 for a sex education course and $150 for the field trips.

But it's just incredible the things you learn in sex education classes. Like, I always thought autoeroticism was parking.

When I was a kid I got all of my information from novels and nothing was explicit. Until I was eighteen years old, I thought you got married, went to Niagara Falls, and asterisked!

I'll never forget the first time I heard the phrase "reproductive organ," I thought it was a pregnant Wurlitzer!

My parents were very strict. When I was eighteen the most daring thing I had ever done was touch a flesh-colored Band-Aid!

What a great slogan for a sex clinic: PATIENTS ARE OUR MOST IMPOTENT PRODUCT!

SHOPPING

THE JONESES RESPOND:
We were the first to have ten-inch TV;
We were the first to have color TV.
You wonder what's next for all to see?
We'll be the first to have bankruptcy.

I just got a phone call from my wife. She said, "On your way home, stop in the store and pick up a package of Cheer." I said, "Procter & Gamble's or Seagram's?"

It's always dangerous to send a husband shopping. Like, who else would take advantage of a special on twenty-five pounds of pepper?

You know what bugs me about department stores? They advertise a carload sale, and no matter how early you get there, nothing is left. I think the car they load is a Volkswagen.

This is an age of specialization. One store sells nothing but chairs, couches, and cushions. It's a headquarters for hindquarters!

You don't know what fear is until you see your wife pushing a shopping cart—through Tiffany's.

My wife loves bargains. Last week she bought me long winter underwear that was irregular—no flap in the back. But it's all right. Fortunately, I'm irregular too!

It's amazing the things people will buy providing they're on sale. For instance, you've heard of electric blankets? Ours is a windup!

Remember when you went into a store, ordered the most expensive item, and said, "The best is none too good"? Now you can say that about almost anything.

SHOW BUSINESS

I haven't heard from my agent in so long, I'm getting worried. Either he died or I did.

I don't want to say anything about my agent, but sometimes I get the feeling he couldn't book the Pope on Sermonette!

Two agents were discussing a comedienne who got married. One agent asked, "What did she do for something old, something new, something borrowed, something blue?" The other agent said, "Her act."

I'm just fascinated by male singers who always have to take off their ties and open their shirts. Tell me, why can't they buy clothes that fit?

I once heard a singer who was so bad, they booked him in Off Key West.

I've always wanted to go up to Marcel Marceau and say, "Ve haf vays to make you talk!"

I just heard a sad story. This girl always wanted to be a ballerina but she had one great handicap—she had a wooden leg. But she wouldn't let this stop her. She studied and trained and practiced and rehearsed—and after ten years she was ready to make her debut with the Royal Ballet. The curtain went up, she tiptoed to center stage, did a fantastic pirouette on her wooden leg—and burned the theater down!

"SHOW ME"

Show me a shoplifted girdle and I'll show you a tax-free foundation.

Show me Mordecai Tupper checking into a motel with Prunella Ware and I'll show you a Tupper-Ware party!

Show me a person who reaches out to his fellow human being—and I'll show you a purse snatcher!

Show me a fella who hasn't memorized his speech and I'll show you the Wizard of Uhs.

SKIING

Skiing has brought joy and happiness and a sense of well-being to hundreds of thousands of people. There is even a name for these people—doctors!

You think I'm kidding? If there was no such thing as skiing, doctors would have invented it!

One of the first things they teach you when skiing is, always keep your knees together. It gives you balance and control, and when you hit something, they don't have to look as far for your shoes.

I was in a class and the girl next to me was having a terrible time—

standing and falling, standing and falling. But she wouldn't give up. She said, "I'm gonna stand on my skis or bust!" The instructor said, "Don't be ridiculous. Just stand on your skis!"

Every time I go to a ski resort I have the same thought: What a great name for a training bra—BEGINNER'S SLOPE!

SMALL TOWNS

I come from a town that's so small, the zip code is a fraction.

It's a very small town. You know how some towns have a godfather? We couldn't afford a godfather. We had a second cousin.

It's the kind of town where the Sunday paper could be delivered by carrier pigeon.

It's a quiet town. If we wanted to have some excitement we'd go down to the hospital and watch them rip off Band-Aids.

This town is so square, a playboy is anyone who stays up to see the eleven o'clock news!

And it was a very poor town. You know how some communities have public washrooms? We had pay bushes!

You would have loved this town. If it wasn't for bowling, there wouldn't have been any culture at all.

I come from a town that believes in law and order. You know how some towns have a cannon in the courthouse square? We had a subpoena!

SMOG

I'll tell you how bad the smog is. I know a six-year-old kid who doesn't believe in three things—Santa Claus, the Easter Bunny, and the sun.

Remember when *Lost Horizon* was a movie? Now it's Los Angeles during a smog alert.

Smog is so bad, this morning I thought I saw a blue jay. It wasn't. It was a cardinal holding its breath.

You know smog is getting to be a problem when a fireman is treated for smoke inhalation—and it's his day off!

Pollution is definitely getting worse. This morning I had to give mouth-to-mouth resuscitation to an air conditioner.

They keep saying the smog situation is getting better but I'm not so sure. Look at Los Angeles. Where else can you find indelible sky-writing?

You've heard of "My Sin"? Now there's a perfume that smells like smog. It's called "Our Sin."

You know something's wrong with the air when your tires start wearing out from the inside.

The smog is so bad in this city, it's ridiculous. Yesterday they caught two people sucking the air out of Canadian tires!

The woman next door really tells it like it is. Yesterday I heard her yelling, "Junior! Don't stand outside. You'll get your lungs all dirty!"

But have you noticed how nobody ever talks about the good side of smog? Do you realize if it wasn't for coughing, some people wouldn't get any exercise at all?

SMOKING

What can you really say about people who smoke three packs a day? They have a heart of gold and fingers to match.

The nice part about smoking three packs a day is, you don't have to worry so much about eating mushrooms.

Actually, smoking and sex have a lot in common. They both give you something to do with your hands.

They now claim that smoking causes wrinkles. So does army coffee.

I quit smoking cold turkey, and you know why? You ever try to keep a cold turkey lit?

Have you heard about the new two-step method to cure yourself of smoking in bed? (1) Buy a water mattress. (2) Fill it with gasoline.

I owe a lot to smoking. Thanks to smoking, I now puff on cigarettes, cigars, pipes, and stairs.

Misery is being a smoker—and being chased by a mugger who isn't.

SNOW

I just saw the abominable snowman. It was a kid who charged me ten dollars to shovel the walk.

That's what kids are charging these days. I call them the Mittens Mafia.

I think this kid was even mentioned in the Bible. It says, "And a little child shall bleed them."

Ten dollars to clear a walk and he's really in demand. I know I called him. You should have heard what I called him!

You know something? When I was a kid, if I had charged someone ten dollars to clear off their walk, I would have wiped my fingerprints off the shovel!

I have to be honest. I can't stand to see my wife shoveling snow. I pull down the shades.

I would have asked my brother-in-law to shovel the snow but, in all fairness, he does have a medical problem—his elbow. He can't get it off the bar.

Once upon a time a middle-aged father sat in his living room and outside it began to snow and snow and snow. Then his big, strong teenage son came into the living room and said, "Gee, Dad, it's beginning to snow and snow and snow!" Whereupon he called up his girl friend, canceled their date for that evening, and without ever being asked, he shoveled all the snow off the driveway, the sidewalk, and the path to the front door. Once upon a time.

Everybody on our street has a snow blower. It's fantastic. We have snow that fell three weeks ago and it still hasn't hit the ground!

Incidentally, do you know the difference between a snow blower and [NAME OF CANDIDATE]? [NAME OF CANDIDATE] throws it all year round.

This should be an interesting winter. My neighbor and I have parallel driveways—and we both bought snow blowers.

SOAP OPERAS

I really don't know much about TV soap operas. To me, "The Secret Storm" is ulcers.

I love those titles—"Search for Tomorrow"! I didn't even know it was missing. Quick, somebody call God!

My wife watches so many soap operas, our picture tube doesn't have snow—it has suds!

My wife loves soap operas. She saves her ironing for them. Every time I smell burnt cloth, I know someone's been either hatched, matched, or dispatched!

Soap operas are marvelous. One show is about an alcoholic, a murderer, a two-timing husband, an embezzler, a teenager on drugs, an unfaithful wife, a child molester, and an unmarried mother. You know what it's called? "Just Plain Folks"!

I won't say what goes on in these stories, but when I change channels, I wear rubber gloves.

They say these soap operas are true to life, which is ridiculous. When did you ever have a thirty-minute argument with your wife that ended with organ music?

But you really get involved. I was watching one today and a father said, "You mean our little Sissie—our sweet, innocent, sheltered, unspoiled daughter—is expecting a baby? Who do you suspect?" Well, I've seen Sissie and I'll tell you who I suspect—the 43rd Armored Cavalry!

And the way these stories drag on. I saw one woman take eleven months to have a premature baby!

I know a soap opera writer who has a terrible problem. His wife said, "Take out the garbage"—and he hasn't sold a script since!

SOCIAL SECURITY

Is there anything more embarrassing than two forty-nine-year-old women meeting in a Social Security office?

Have you seen the estimates of what we'll be paying for Social Security in the future? Congress thinks of everything. Not only does the government take care of you in your old age—but it makes you reach it a lot faster.

My neighbor's a real conservative. He says the only Social Security he ever needed was a diaper.

SONS

I have a son who needs orthodonture, his tonsils taken out, glasses, and orthopedic shoes. It's like I told my wife, "This is the last kid we take 'as is'!"

What's more, he's a hypochondriac. Five times a day I have to tell him there is no such thing as terminal acne!

Kids today have it made. My kid has his own room, his own TV, his own stereo, his own library, his own refrigerator. When he wants to run away from home he doesn't pack a suitcase, he calls Allied!

My kids are always on the defensive. One morning I shook my ten-year-old and said, "Wake up. I want to show you something." He said, "What?" I said, "The break of day." He said, "I wasn't near it!"

Have you noticed how kids are always complaining? To a five-year-old, nothing is ever right. He's like Ralph Nader with a runny nose!

I was telling my boss about the upsetting thing that happened at our house today. The dogcatcher got Rex. He said, "Rex is your dog?" I said, "Rex is our son."

There's something unnerving about a kid with a Daniel Boone haircut, a Mark Twain mustache, and an Abe Lincoln beard telling you he's rejecting the past.

I have a fourteen-year-old son who has so much hair, I don't know whether to call him Melvin or Rapunzel.

I'll tell you how long my son's hair is. It's been three years since we bought him a haircut, a tie, or jockey shorts.

My wife gets so sentimental about our teenager. Last week she went out and bronzed his parole.

I don't want to brag about my kids but my son is a four-letter student in high school and it's going to save me a fortune in college. The four letters are D-U-M-B and he isn't going!

Kids today are very concerned about ecology. Yesterday my teenager said, "We have to do something about cleaning up the environment!" I said, "Great! Let's start with your room!"

You should see his room—and he won't let anyone touch it. He says, "Leave it alone. I know where everything is." And he does. It's on the floor!

You've never seen such a mess. One time we brought in a vacuum cleaner and it threw up!

My wife keeps worrying about cockroaches. I said, "Cockroaches? You think a cockroach would go in there? Never in the history of the world has there been a kamikaze cockroach!"

One time I got so fed up, I gave him five dollars and said, "Here! Take this and I don't ever want to see a mess like this again!" So he took the five dollars and I have never seen a mess like that again. He bought a lock for the door!

SPEAKERS

People who are called upon to make their first public speech—writhe to the occasion.

What a great slogan for a German public-speaking school: WE HAVE WAYS TO MAKE YOU TALK!

_____ isn't the most dynamic speaker in the world. I heard one of his talks. It was halfway between tax reform and chloroform.

Most public speakers know the precise moment their audience loses interest. It's twenty-five minutes before they stop.

If you're a speaker, the communication gap is half your audience yawning.

I didn't say he gives a deadly talk. I just said he's the only man I know who has a black belt for speaking.

He couldn't get a standing ovation if he closed with "The Star-Spangled Banner."

The credibility gap is when the moderator says it will be a very short commencement speech—and then Howard Cosell gets up to give it.

Some speeches are like broiled lobster. You have to pick through an awful lot to find any meat.

SPEAKERS' "AD LIBS"

I have a very sobering statement to make. The bar closes in fifteen minutes.

I wouldn't mind being the first speaker tonight if it wasn't for something the master of ceremonies told me during dinner. He said he likes to start off each program with a joke. Then he introduced *me!*

ACKNOWLEDGING A HUMOROUS INTRODUCTION: That's what I call an acupuncture introduction. One needle after another.

ACKNOWLEDGING A HUMOROUS INTRODUCTION: Now I know why they call him a toastmaster. Toast—that's a square with a lot of crust.

ACKNOWLEDGING YOUR INTRODUCTION: That was a very touching introduction. So was being introduced to your finance chairman.

ACKNOWLEDGING YOUR INTRODUCTION: I want to thank Mr. _____ for that kind, generous, I might even say lavish, introduction. For a while there I wasn't sure if I was ten feet tall or six feet under.

ACKNOWLEDGING YOUR INTRODUCTION: I want to thank you for that glowing introduction. I think some of the statements in it were overly generous—but as a golfer, I'm always grateful for a good lie.

AFTER A DEAD MICROPHONE IS REPAIRED: I'm glad you fixed that. For a while there I was beginning to feel like Marcel Marceau.

AFTER A LONG PAUSE: In public speaking there's an old expression. He who hesitates has lost his place.

AFTER QUOTING STATISTICS: I realize those are rather startling statistics. I can see three people out there with their mouths open [MIME YAWNING AND COVERING YOUR MOUTH].

AFTER USING A VERY BIG WORD: I'm sorry but I'm crazy about using big words. There's even a name for it—psychosemantic.

ANSWERING AN ANGRY REMARK: Sir, it really wouldn't be fair for me to argue with you because you've lost your head—and your brains are in it.

ANSWERING CRITICISM: Wait a minute. I hear something. I think it's the fermentation of sour grapes!

COMPLAINT: Sir, we are what we eat. I know that because I just saw you taking a pill.

DEBATE: Tonight we have one speaker for and one speaker against. It's like stereo. You'll be getting it from both sides.

FOLLOWING UP A SPEECH: I haven't been so choked up since my dentist gave a talk entitled ADVENTURES IN DENTURES.

IF SOMEBODY LEAVES DURING YOUR SPEECH, CALL AFTER THEM: I might get better! . . . Something like that used to make me very insecure, but no more. [STICK YOUR THUMB IN YOUR MOUTH.]

IF THE MICROPHONE IS TOO LOW: Who were you expecting—Mickey Rooney?

IF THERE IS A DELAY IN YOUR SPEECH: As you can see, I don't exactly stop the show, but I do slow it up.

IF YOU ARE IN AN EMBARRASSING SITUATION: I wouldn't give this spot to a dermatologist.

IF YOU BECOME CONFUSED: I'm sorry. I lost my train of thought—and it wasn't an express to begin with.

IF YOU FORGET SOMETHING: I have a photographic memory. It's just that sometimes I forget to take off the lens cap!

IF YOU HAVE A PROBLEM AT THE START: As you might have noticed, this is my fish market speech. For the first few minutes I flounder.

IF YOU LOSE YOUR PLACE: You'll have to excuse me. I have so much editing, cross-outs, and changes in this, I call it my repaired text.

INTERMISSION: We will now have a fifteen-minute break. In the words of that wonderful old spiritual: LET MY PEOPLE GO!

INTERRUPTER: Sir, may I say to you those four words that have been made so popular by the phone company: "You're out of order!"

INTERRUPTER: Sir, our time is flying and you're trying to hijack it.

INVOLVED QUESTION: Sir, could you tell this story a little faster? I don't quite know how to put this but your tale is dragging.

LARYNGITIS: Laryngitis can get you into a lot of trouble. All day long I've been talking in a whisper and I knew I had this speech tonight, so I called up [NAME OF MODERATOR] to tell him about it and his wife answered the phone. And that's when I found out that laryngitis can get you into a lot of trouble. I said [WHISPERING], "Is [FIRST NAME OF MODERATOR] home?" She said [ALSO WHISPERING], "No. Come on over!"

NERVOUSNESS: As I stand here before this distinguished audience, I don't know which is knocking more—opportunity or my knees.

NERVOUS PARTICIPANT: You're so nervous. You look like Evel Knievel's insurance man.

NOISY GROUP: You look at that table and you know what's wrong with the world—ten speakers and no listeners.

NOISY GUEST: Sir, I'd like to give you a going-away present. But you've got to do your part.

REBUTTAL: You've got a point there—and if you put your hat on, nobody will notice it.

REBUTTAL: I couldn't swallow that if it came with a chaser!

REBUTTAL: That's a very meaty question and I'd like to give it a very meaty answer—baloney!

SMALL AUDIENCE: I haven't seen anything this empty since I looked in the suggestion box at the Kremlin.

TO SOMEBODY INTERRUPTING: Sir, I wouldn't mind your mini-brain if it wasn't for your maxi-mouth!

WHEN A JOKE DIES: If silence is golden, that joke has got to be worth $42,000!

WHEN A MEMBER OF THE AUDIENCE GIVES A SPEECH INSTEAD OF ASKING A QUESTION: Sir, would you mind just phrasing your question? Our lease is up in January.

WHEN AUDIENCE REACTS TO A BEAUTIFUL GIRL: I second the emotion.

WHEN SOMEBODY ASKS A VERY PERTINENT QUESTION: Sir, I hope you're married—because that is a very pregnant question.

WHEN SOMEBODY GOOFS YOUR INTRODUCTION: It could be worse. Last week a master of ceremonies introduced me by saying, "And now we bring you the latest dope from Hollywood!" [SUBSTITUTE YOUR CITY.]

WHEN SOMEONE ASKS A TRICK QUESTION: Sir, I just want to know if you have a permit to carry that loaded question.

WHEN SOMEONE SAYS, "CAN'T YOU TAKE A JOKE?": Of course I can. Where do you want to go?

WHEN SOMETHING GOES WRONG: Don't worry. This is all part of the program. This is the part we didn't practice.

WHEN SPEAKING TO AN AUDIENCE OF EXPERTS: First let me say I'm well aware of the fact that many of you out there are better qualified to deal with this subject than I am. Better qualified? I feel like I'm giving a talk on flood control to Noah!

WHEN THE LIGHTS GO OUT: It's a pleasure to be here on this extinguished occasion.

WHEN THE MICROPHONE DOESN'T WORK: I don't really need the microphone. I'm used to talking loud. I have three kids, a dog, and a stereo.

WHEN THE MICROPHONE DOESN'T WORK: Could we get an electrician? The microphone is on the bum and it should be the other way around.

WHEN THE SOUND SYSTEM DOESN'T WORK: I don't know why they call these things a P.A. system. To me they're always P.U.

WHEN YOU DROP YOUR PAPERS: I've heard of a speech falling flat, but this is ridiculous!

WHEN YOU GARBLE WORDING: I was born with a silver spoon in my mouth and sometimes I think it's still there!

WHEN YOU PUT ON GLASSES: I don't really need these glasses. I just use them to find things—like my office.

WHEN YOU QUOTE: At this point I'd like to say a few appropriated words.

WHEN YOU'RE IN A LARGE MEETING HALL: Isn't this a wonderful room? I think they used it for the creditors of [BANKRUPT FIRM IN YOUR FIELD].

WHEN YOU STOP FOR A SIP OF WATER: As you can see, this is a prepared speech. All you add is water.

WHEN YOU TAKE A LONG TIME ADJUSTING THE MICROPHONE: Forgive me but it's really necessary. I'm one of those Teddy Roosevelt talkers. I speak softly and carry a big microphone! I always have trouble with these things. One time I was giving a speech and the toastmaster leaned over and said, "You're too close to the microphone." So I moved back a little, continued with my speech, and five minutes later he leaned over again and said, "You're still too close to the microphone." I said, "How far away should I be?" He said, "Got a car?"

WHILE PUTTING ON YOUR GLASSES: Some people say they don't really need these things. I do. Whenever anybody sings, "Oh, say can you see?"—my answer is, "No!"

YOUNG, CONSERVATIVE AUDIENCE: As I stand here looking into your well-scrubbed faces, your short haircuts, and your closely trimmed sideburns—one thought crossed my mind: Some people will do anything to get attention!

SPEAKERS' COMMENTS

It's a great honor to be here tonight after having satisfied the two philosophical requirements of your Program Committee. The two philosophical requirements: (1) They believe in free speech. And (2) They believe in free speeches.

Next month we'll be having our annual Beef-Stew New Year's Eve Party. The dinner will be beef and the diners will be stewed.

We have a very modest, outgoing chairman but I happen to know that, during his term of office, he sat through dozens of debates. He sat through scores of planning sessions. And he sat through hundreds of meetings. In fact, one time I asked him, "If I was picked to be the next chairman, what preparation would I need?" He said, "Hi!"

I said, "Before you go any further, I'd like to say one thing." He said, "What's that?" I said, "Don't go any further!"

I had an interesting experience coming in from the airport. The driver thought this hotel was in Tipperary. He kept taking the long way.

I haven't exactly made the greatest impression in my field. You've heard of *Who's Who?* I'm in *Who He?*

As I look out over this assembly and realize that we represent the finest minds and talent our profession has to offer—before we begin I'd like to ask Reverend Jones to say a short prayer for our country.

Actually, I was feeling pretty good until I peeked through the curtain and saw how many of you were here tonight. Then I was suddenly taken sober!

I once went to a seminar where the cocktail hour ran from three to seven. When I answered questions from the floor, you better believe it!

Please excuse me if I'm a little nervous tonight. I've been to many speeches as a member of the audience, but this is the first time I've ever stood up here—on the windward side.

You can't blame me for being nervous. I live in a high-risk neighborhood—Earth!

[TAKE OFF YOUR WATCH AND PUT IT ON THE LECTERN.] Don't let that reassure you. It's a sundial.

Most speakers feel that 50 percent is what you deliver and 50 percent is how you deliver it. Masters and Johnson feel the same way.

The program chairman told me the essence of a good speech is to have a beginning and an end, and keep the two as close together as possible. . . . So in conclusion . . .

It's never a good idea to give a very long speech. One time I gave a two-hour talk, and when it was over, the audience rose to its feet and cried, "Bully! Bully!" But they were so tired, they kept leaving off the Y.

This will be a rather short talk tonight and you can thank three people for it. My partner, who took a forty-five-minute speech and edited it down to thirty minutes. My wife, who took the thirty-minute speech and edited it down to fifteen minutes. And my secretary, who took the fifteen-minute speech and lost it.

This was originally a forty-five-minute speech but thanks to what my wife said last night, it's only a fifteen-minute speech. She said what she always says at night: "Take out the garbage!"

I'd like to move this right along—before my welcome wears out and the martinis wear off.

I'll tell you what started me giving short speeches. One time I was giving a real long one and I heard these two fellas talking in the front row. One nudged the other and said, "Do you figure he's heading for the finish?" And his friend answered, "Only if he makes a U-turn!"

In many ways, a speaker is faced with the same problem a bridegroom has on his wedding night. Everybody knows what he's there for. The big question is: "Can he deliver?"

And now I'd like to depart from the prepared text and say something I can understand too.

I have a ten-minute talk and a twenty-minute talk. It's the same talk. I lose my place a lot.

I may seem a little disorganized but I'm really not. I'm like a swizzle stick. I do my best work when going around in circles.

I've done so much after-dinner speaking in the last few years, all I have to do is see a slice of roast beef and I start feeling for my notes.

As a public speaker, I like to think I have a stake in the future. I'm getting mighty sick of chicken à la king!

It's a pleasure to be talking to such a large group. I gave a speech last night. The audience was so small, when they applauded it sounded like three nudists sitting on a marble bench!

I'll tell you how I did. I got a shrugging ovation.

We've had such quiet audiences, you know how some shows have signs saying LAUGH and APPLAUD? We have signs saying INHALE and EXHALE.

I call this my no-bra speech. A point here, a point there, but in between it's kind of shaky.

Air pollution is getting worse. You can tell. Last night I gave a speech, and by the time I finished, half the audience were holding their noses.

People say the most interesting things after speeches. One time a little old lady came up to me and said, "Mr. [YOUR NAME], some speeches give me food for thought." I said, "Yes?" She said, "Yours was more like a canapé."

You have to watch out for little old ladies. Last week one of them came up to me after a talk and said, "Mr. [YOUR NAME], you may find this hard to believe, but your speech reminded me of a little dog I have at home." I said, "Isn't that sweet! My speech reminded you of a little dog you have at home? What kind of dog?" She said, "Bull!"

We had a great audience last night. They specialized in group yawning.

You've been such a great audience, I hate to break this up. What say we all go down to a health food store and watch the bread mold?

And now we come to the part of our program that every husband who has ever come home at three o'clock in the morning is familiar with—the question and answer period.

Before we take a ten-minute break, I would like to leave you with this thought: He who hesitates—will stand on a mighty long line in the washroom!

I want to thank you for that staring ovation.

I'll try to keep this simple because I put theories in the same category as pigeons. I don't want to have anything to do with them when they're over my head.

You know what I like about this group? It really gets down to business. We've covered more ground than a Weight Watchers picnic!

I talked to a wild group last night. I knew it the minute someone yelled "Louder!" during the silent meditation.

This is more laughs than the men's room in the Leaning Tower of Pisa.

We will now sing that grand old favorite: "Don't Listen to the Mississippi River, Grandma, It Has a Dirty Mouth!"

I haven't heard that dirty a laugh since I asked the man at the Post Office to mark a package FRAGILE.

Would the owner of a blue Pontiac with license plate XYZ-123 please report to the parking lot? The attendant has good news and bad news for you. The good news is that your headlights are on. The bad news is *what* your headlights are on—the ground!

The worst announcement you can ever hear is: "Will the owner of a blue Buick please report to the parking lot. The license plate *used* to be 4Y-1893!"

I'm so tired of being so handsome, attractive, and irresistible to girls —I may just get the world's first bald transplant.

My competitor has said we ought to take the bull by the horns and he may be right. He's a lot more familiar with bull than I am.

SPORTS

I just joined a tennis club and I've never been so disappointed. I thought mixed doubles was wife-swapping.

There are certain rules about skydiving you should always keep in mind. Like, never have an argument with your wife while she's packing your chute.

Did you read about the sky diver who asked for instructions on how to use the parachute? The instructor told him, "You count to ten and pull the rip cord." The sky diver said, "W-w-w-w-what w-w-w-w-w-was th-th-th-th-that n-n-n-n-n-n-number a-a-again?" The instructor said, "Three."

Nineteen seventy-nine is the year I learned how to play golf. It was also my score.

When I play golf I have a lot of style but I don't hit the ball far enough. What I'm trying to say is—I know how to address the ball; I just don't put enough stamps on it!

SPRING

I just saw the first sign of spring—a beautiful green hillside and, against it, a cluster of yellow bulldozers.

Spring is here—when nature sends out her Buds in six-packs!

Spring is when the furnace repairmen leave for the French Riviera and the air-conditioning repairmen return.

Spring really gets the vital juices flowing. I just saw two senior citizens standing in front of an X-rated movie singing, "Memories. Memories!"

You can always tell when spring is here by subtle little signs—like, when you start your car in the morning, it does.

STOCKBROKERS

I'm beginning to wonder about my broker. Yesterday I told him to buy a hundred shares of A.T.&T. He said, "Would you spell that?"

My broker keeps talking about things like "the breadth of the market." To me it's always been bad.

When I first went to him he said, "Don't worry. You're at the end of your financial troubles." Six months later I'm out $10,000. So I went back to him and said, "I thought you said I was at the end of my financial troubles." He said, "I did. I just didn't say which end!"

I'll tell you when I started to question this broker. There's nothing wrong with putting $500,000 into a maternity hospital—but in Sun City?

My broker has a peculiar sense of humor. This morning he called me up and said, "I have good news and bad news. The Dow Jones is down thirty points, your portfolio is down forty points, and if you don't come up with $50,000 to cover margin, we're selling you out! —And now, the bad news."

STOCK MARKET

The minister of a church in the financial district closed his sermon with, "Keep one thing in mind: There will be no buying and selling of securities in heaven!" One parishioner leaned over to another and said, "It doesn't matter. That ain't where the stock market is going."

Last week I put half my money in the stock market and half I spent foolishly. Now I'm not sure which half.

Isn't this a fantastic market? Up, down, up, down— and that's just my stomach!

I'm so nervous, yesterday I got a fingernail transplant!

Nowadays an investor is someone who stands with both feet firmly on the ground—and his portfolio in it.

I take a philosophical view of things. Like, if God had intended us to be rich, he never would have given us the stock market.

My mother taught me never to get mixed up with bad company. So did the stock market.

One of the first things you learn in the stock market is never listen to anyone who writes out a system to make $1 million in three months —on the back of his unemployment check.

I've been so unlucky in the stock market, if life begins at forty, I would have bought it at eighty-seven.

I have a Marie Antoinette approach to the stock market. When things look bad, I lose my head.

The stock market is like the Chinese water torture.
A lot of little drops can drive you crazy!

Personally, I have a Zen philosophy about the stock market. I started off with $10,000—and Zen I had $8,000, and Zen I had $5,000, and Zen I had . . .

Talk about unusual business gifts, they now have flesh-colored Band-Aids for people who got out of the stock market. They're yellow.

Everybody's talking about another 1929. Shakespeare even wrote a play about 1929: *The Taming of the Shrewd.*

They say 1980 is a leap year. So was 1929.

I feel the same way about the stock market as I do about driving. It would be a lot of fun if it wasn't for an occasional crash.

Do you ever get the impression that 1929 is being recycled?

Think positively. If the Dow-Jones Average drops ninety-two points in one day, look at all the money you'll save on prune juice.

They say the stock market is having a technical reaction. That's right. It can tech every nical you've got!

I've been having a terrible time in the stock market. Last week my portfolio went down $800—and this was on a Sunday!

I won't say how I've done in the stock market but my wife says we're the only family on our street with a breadloser.

I have one of those diversified portfolios. I'm 20 percent in utilities, 30 percent in oils, 50 percent in electronics, and 100 percent in hock.

Three years ago I bought a no-load mutual fund and I finally figured out what the no-load refers to—my wallet.

I specialize in Sweet Chariot stocks. The minute I buy them they swing low!

I don't want to complain, but I just wish my blood pressure was going down like my stocks are.

I don't know why, but every morning my stocks open lower. I think I have the only companies that go dump in the night.

Some stocks split. Mine just crumble.

I have a diversified portfolio—50 percent are stocks and 50 percent are bombs.

I always buy those breakfast cereal stocks. They go snap, crackle, and drop!

Isn't this a marvelous technological age we're living in? We now have two things that are self-cleaning—ovens and the stock market.

SUMMER CAMP

Laugh and the world laughs with you; cry and you have five kids home for the summer.

There are four things you can do to make this a summer your kids will never forget. Send them to a camp that has planned, nutritious meals; that has a varied sports and athletic program; that has trained, understanding counselors; and when you've done all this—MOVE!

When you write away for information about a summer camp, five days later you get back a folder showing this lovely ninety-acre estate with two swimming pools, tennis courts, riding stables, and a private lake. The first thing you should understand is, this is not the camp. It's the owner's home. . . . The camp itself is a converted Exxon station!

You have to be very wary of these brochures. They use phrases like "mature leadership." That means the counselors' pimples have cleared up.

Another wonderful phrase is "body-building food." That means mashed potatoes, macaroni, rice, and baked beans three times a day. I don't know whose body they're trying to build but I think it's Jackie Gleason's!

My kid ate so much mashed potatoes and macaroni, on a hot day he starched his own shirts!

You can't believe how luxurious some of these camps are. It's the first time I ever saw a tent with a chandelier.

I know one summer camp that's so expensive they have Cadillac canoes!

My kid goes to one of those camps where they really rough it. The TV is black and white.

"It is better to have loved and lost." I'll tell you who said that. A father who got the bill from summer camp.

Summer camps are where kids make wallets and empty their fathers'.

Every year I used to watch my wife spend days sewing name tapes into our son's clothes. No more. We just changed his name to Machine Washable.

The most important thing when you send your kid to camp is to make sure he has name tapes in all his clothes. If he doesn't have name tapes, they'll call him by any label they can find. Last year, for two whole months, one kid was known as Fruit of the Loom!

The whole idea of summer camp is the buddy system. You do everything with another kid. You walk together, you talk together, you eat together—for six weeks. It's like a Hollywood marriage, only longer!

I was always unlucky at summer camp. I'll tell you what I mean. You ever share a sleeping bag with a bed wetter? . . . Other kids had a pillow. I had a life preserver!

There's a real science to summer camps. For instance, they always have the girls camp on the other side of the lake. This teaches the boys three things: discipline, self-control, and swimming!

So far he's been gone three weeks and all we've received from him is one postcard—asking if fingers can be transplanted.

July is when you can always tell the experienced parents. They get a letter from their kid in summer camp saying four things are going around—chicken pox, measles, mumps, and bubonic plague—and they send him two aspirin.

One time we went up to visit him and his face was covered with lumps. I said, "What is it? Mumps?" He said, "No. I'm the receiver on the baseball team." I said, "You mean the catcher." He said, "Sometimes."

And summer camps are very educational. Thanks to summer camps, kids have no trouble recognizing poison ivy. It's what's under the bandages.

Kids always pick the perfect psychological moment to tell you they have poison ivy. It's right after they shake your hand.

That may sound funny to you but the most difficult thing to explain to a wife is why your son has poison ivy, why you have poison ivy, and why your secretary has poison ivy.

And summer camps teach you other practical things, like how to find your way home when you're lost in the woods. You don't know how helpful that is to a kid who lives on Seventy-third Street and Lexington Avenue.

Summer camps are where kids go to change their attitudes, their habits, their routines—everything but their underwear.

My kid swears he takes a bath every Saturday night. If that's so, he must be drinking it.

When it comes to not taking baths, even for summer camps my kid is exceptional. When I asked for directions to his tent, they said, "Just follow your nose!"

You go into his tent and there are mosquitoes all over the floor. Who can fly with one hand holding your nose?

My wife said, "When he gets home we're going to need strong soap." I said, "Are you kidding? When he gets home we're going to need Oven Off!"

Every year when the kids come back from camp, we celebrate by having our annual barbecue. First, we set fire to something that's small, hard, and black—their socks.

A lot of people say that kids today are spoiled. Well, let me set your mind at ease. Kids today are not spoiled. It's just the way they smell after six weeks at summer camp.

My three kids were at the breakfast table this morning and I said to my wife, "It seems like only yesterday they left for summer camp." She said, "It was only yesterday. They got on the wrong bus."

It's amazing the way kids change when they're away for a few months. If the doorbell rings and someone calls you "Dad," don't take any chances. Check the name tape!

My teenager came home three inches taller. I'll explain how he did that. I told him that every morning he should put on a clean pair of socks. Next time I'll tell him to take off the old ones first!

SUMMER JOBS

Summertime and the living is easy. Not if you sell snowmobiles.

My son wants me to find him a summer job. He asked me to check with my boss, my friends, my business associates. Then he asked me to run off 100 copies of a résumé, call up the employment agencies, and write an ad for the POSITIONS WANTED section of the newspaper. I asked him what he wanted to call himself in the ad. He said, "A self-starter!"

Kids today want to make a hundred dollars a week on a summer job. A hundred dollars a week! When I was a kid, the only people in town who made a hundred dollars a week were a working couple— Bonnie and Clyde!

I asked my son, "What can you do?" He said, "Nothing." I said, "Good. I'll get you a job in the government. They won't have to break you in."

No, I'm only kidding. Kids today aren't afraid of hard work. Kids aren't afraid of hard work for the same reason I'm not afraid of an African lion. They never get too close to it.

SUPERMARKETS

Ingenuity is what has made America great. One day I was on the speed checkout line at the supermarket. The checker said to the woman in front of me, "I'm sorry, madam, but you have twenty-four items. This line is for carts with eight items or less." She said, "Wait a minute"—and got two more carts.

I don't know who's running the express line at the local supermarket but I think it's Amtrak.

Something's got to give. I mean, I don't mind spending forty-two dollars at the supermarket—but on the express line?

This fella went into a police station and said, "My wife drew $5,000 out of the bank and I think she ran away." The desk sergeant said, "She drew $5,000 out of the bank? Weren't you suspicious?" He said, "No. She said she was going to the supermarket."

Nowadays the easiest way to break a fifty-dollar bill is to drop it on a checkout counter.

It's terrible. Yesterday hijackers stole $10,000 worth of groceries from a supermarket. Got away in a Volkswagen.

But the stores are really trying. They now have something that lets you get three meals out of one pound of hamburger—the price.

Ladies, I have a great way to save money when you next go shopping: Chop meat! Chop meat right off your shopping list.

STAKEOUT: What you say when you see the price of beef.

And it isn't just meat. Remember when a buccaneer was a pirate? Now it's the price of corn.

Do you know what they're getting for things like cornflakes and puffed rice? They're called dry cereals. Not anymore. I cry all over them!

You can always tell the newlyweds in a supermarket. They're the ones who squeeze the breakfast cereal boxes to see if they're fresh!

I just want to know what the government is doing about the biggest financial problem of them all—the peso! Every time we go into a supermarket, why do we have to peso much?

You can put on airs everywhere else but in a supermarket you have to act your wage.

Food is so expensive, anyone who burps is a liar!

I'll tell you how fast money goes. I just saw a shopping cart with a racing stripe.

Our grocery bills have been running eighty dollars a week. I told my wife, "Don't give me any of that inflation stuff! Somewhere you've got a 500-pound lover!"

This morning my wife said she had a plan that could cut our food bills in half. I said, "That's great! What is it?" She said, "Alternate side of the table eating!"

I'll tell you how high prices are. I just saw a butcher's bill with a nosebleed.

SWINGERS

I was having a marvelous time in a mate-swapping club until the government loused it up. They passed the truth-in-lending law.

From an efficiency standpoint you just can't beat a mate-swapping club. It has no dues—and very few don'ts!

I can remember when suburban couples would get together for an evening and swap tales. Come to think of it, they still do.

I'm not what you might call a swinger. You're looking at the only fella who ever went to an orgy and played charades.

Nowadays many girls offer you sex on a silver platter—which is a wild way to get the tarnish off.

TALK SHOWS

We've always had sex education, only it was called by a different name—TV talk shows.

You hear the wildest conversations on talk shows. Like:
"Every day I look at thousands of naked legs and breasts."
"You're a producer?"
"No. Colonel Sanders."

I hear things on these shows Krafft wouldn't have said to Ebing!

TAXES

I never worry about the future. High interest rates have taught me how to live within my income—and high taxes have taught me how to live without my income.

Thanks to federal, state, county, and city taxes, if you make $50,000 a year it doesn't mean you *have* money. It means you *had* money.

There's only one problem with soaking the rich—a little of the detergent gets on everyone!

I don't want to complain but every time they build a tax structure, the first thing they nail is *me!*

It's fantastic how many taxes there are. Property taxes, sales taxes, income taxes. They even have taxes on taxicabs and prune juice. They get you coming and going!

We have a bedbug system of taxation. It's amazing how many different ways they put the bite on you.

In this city a man's home is his castle. It looks like a home and it's taxed like a castle.

Taxes are now so high, this morning a neighbor came over and wanted to borrow a cup of something—money!

TEENAGERS

There are only two ways to successfully cope with teenagers: self-control now or birth control then.

You know that having a calm, reasoned, tranquil discussion with your teenager is in vain—when one of them starts to stick out on your forehead.

A teenager is someone who borrows ten dollars, your new leather coat, and the keys to the car, to take his girl to a lecture on the simple life.

A teenager is someone who calls his parents squares—and then travels fifty-five miles to see a Jack Oakie Film Festival.

When your kids come home at two o'clock in the morning and you ask them where they were, here's how you can tell if they're lying: Are their mouths open?

I just heard my first teenager work song. It's all about sweating and straining and pulling and ripping and cutting and slashing and tearing and lifting. It's called "Opening Up the Letter with That No-good Check from Home."

Let's face it. The only time teenagers put their shoulders to the wheel is when they neck in a Volkswagen!

I have a fifteen-year-old kid who's always saying, "I have a mind of my own!" When I was fifteen I didn't even have a bed of my own!

They say teenagers are smarter than ever so I asked mine to do something about the snow on the front walk. Well sir—that vacuum cleaner will never be the same!

I have a question. Millions of kids are searching for their identity. Why is it the first place they look is in the refrigerator?

I know a teenager who got July and August as a summer vacation. So she went into the bathroom to fix her hair. Then in August . . .

A lot of kids want to replace "The Star-Spangled Banner" as our national anthem. It starts off with "Oh, say can you see?"—and with their haircuts, the answer is "No!"

Teenage haircuts come in three different styles: LONG, LONGER, and PARDON ME, SIR, BUT YOU'RE STANDING ON MY SIDEBURNS!

Teenagers today have the sofa look. All they want is mohair.

Have you noticed the way kids dress today? One father said to his wife, "Dear, I looked at our daughter today and I think she has a drug problem." She said, "Drug as in marijuana?" He said, "No. Drug as in by the cat!"

I can remember when teenage girls were called dreamboats. Now they look more like tramp steamers.

TELEPHONES

Do you realize if Alexander Graham Bell hadn't invented the telephone, we'd all be sitting around waiting for the bridge lamp to ring?

I can't understand the telephone company. I came up with a great idea to make life simpler for telephone users and it's just ignoring it. A directory for unlisted numbers!

I don't know why people are always knocking the phone company. I can get dial tones without any trouble—usually halfway through my calls.

I've always found it significant that when you lose a coin, the phone company sends you stamps. Do you think it's saying, maybe you ought to write a letter?

Breathes there a man so free from greed
That never has he felt the need,
When in a phone booth, to explore
The coin return slot just once more?

Did you know the telephone company is now using men as operators? Neither did I until I got one on the phone. I said, "I'd like to talk to an operator." He said, "I am an operator." I said, "How do I know you're an operator?" He said, "I'm alone with eighty-five women, aren't I?"

Personally, I think the phone company should add a little sex appeal to its operation. Like calling the girls in Directory Assistance—informaniacs!

Yesterday I got a phone call and a low sexy voice said, "I want your body!" What a sneaky way to collect blood for the Red Cross!

My uncle got two years in jail because of a wrong number. It was on his income tax.

A loser is someone who phones a number on a washroom wall—and it's Dial-A-Prayer!

I know a fella who makes obscene phone calls. He calls up Christian Scientists and says, "Penicillin, antibiotics, cortisone, aspirin!"

I like to think deep philosophical thoughts—like, how does an obscene caller know when he gets a wrong number?

I just heard the weirdest conversation. My secretary answered a ring and it was an obscene caller. She said, "I'm very busy. Would you mind hurrying it up?" He said, "I'm breathing as fast as I can!"

TELEVISION

TV is one tube it's mighty hard to squeeze anything good out of.

Television is the device that brings people into your living you wouldn't have in your living room.

People will watch anything on television. I can prove it. You know that little white spot that appears when you turn off the set? Last week it got an 18.2 Nielsen!

People are funny. If friends lied to us as much as our TV set does, we'd have nothing to do with them.

Do you get the feeling that this season, television is hitting new highs in lows?

They say there's nothing new under the sun. I just saw the new prime-time TV programs. There's nothing new under the moon either.

What do I think of the new television shows? Well, I now have a callus from changing stations.

I don't want to complain about the new TV season, but I've gone from Channel 2 to Channel 4 to Channel 6 to Seagram 7.

Some of the TV heroes this season are so old it's embarrassing. One of them has to take two Anacin just to make a fist.

If somebody says, "Reach!"—it's for a Social Security check!

I saw one show that was so bad, I think it was done in living duller.

I won't say what the new shows are like but it's the first time I ever saw a TV repairman back in.

Show me the man who laughs when things go wrong and I'll show you a TV repairman!

TV is when you give a repairman forty-two dollars to replace a tube worth three dollars so you can watch a show that says, "Crime doesn't pay."

I know a fella who never pays any attention to the shade of a man's skin. Unfortunately, he's the one who fixes my color TV set.

Have you noticed how most of the new TV shows come in one color —mediocher?

This season the accent is on total frankness in language, approach, and subject matter. I knew it the minute *TV Guide* showed up in a plain brown wrapper.

You have no idea what's happening on these programs. I can remember when HORIZONTAL HOLD was a little knob around on the side of the set. Now it's a little fooling around on the front of it.

It's embarrassing. One show is about a doctor who becomes sexually involved with one of his patients. What makes it so embarrassing, he's a tree surgeon.

I was telling my secretary they want to do a TV special about me as the sex symbol of the year. All they need is a title. She said, "How about 'He? Haw!'"

I know a newlywed who's very upset with television. She says, "The trouble with TV is, it's either sex or violence." I said, "What do you mean sex or violence?" She said, "If you turn it on, it's violence. If you turn it off, it's sex!"

I don't want to put down the new TV series but in my neighborhood we've always had something that shows us crime, corruption, lawbreaking, and violence. It's called a window.

Blaming TV for violence is like blaming beds for sex.

In our neighborhood, cable TV is when the set is chained to the radiator.

They go so fast. I had one set disappear between "Here's" and "Johnny"!

Personally, I'd like to see more TV shows with the accent on entertainment. Like sixty minutes of Dolly Parton with the hiccups!

I love the old movies on TV. Last night I saw the one where Cary Grant plays a cat burglar. Remember that one? In the very first scene he steals three cats!

"The evil that men do lives after them." I didn't believe it until I saw a rerun on TV.

You know who loves to watch TV? My dog. That's right. When Oral Roberts says, "Heal!"—he goes out of his mind!

Did you know that Henny Youngman was the inspiration for 'Sesame Street'? "A guy comes up to me on the street and Sesame . . ."

Magic is watching TV with three little kids in the room. Now you see it; now you don't!

If inflation, crime, poverty, unemployment, and war are eliminated, can you imagine the profound change it's going to make in our lives? For instance, in the future, the first ten minutes of the seven o'clock news will be a dance act.

TELEVISION COMMERCIALS

You have no idea how frank these TV medical shows are. I saw one that covered abortion, leprosy, and venereal disease. It's the first time I ever enjoyed a sinus commercial.

Headache commercials are always talking about fast, fast relief. What fast? It takes an hour just to get the cotton out of the bottle!

The commercials on television are a little like watching those old army training films. I've never seen so many things I could do without.

I love to watch A *Christmas Carol* on TV because it's so honest. They show four commercials and then Scrooge says, "Humbug!"

I'll never forget the first time I discovered I was middle-aged. It was the day they showed a TV commercial for heartburn, nagging backache, and falling hair—and I realized I was listening to it.

I love to watch the commercials on television: "I get seventy-five dollars a week in extra cash when I'm in the hospital!" "How do you do that?" "I mug doctors!"

THANKSGIVING

Be honest now. Don't those big balloons in the Thanksgiving Day Parade remind you of one of the candidates? Hot air entirely surrounded by a very thin skin?

Thanksgiving is when the frost is on the pumpkin and the corn is in shock—at what butchers are asking for turkeys!

All you have to do is ask your butcher what he's charging a pound and you'll know that turkeys aren't the only ones who are getting it in the neck!

Don't you just hate people who show off? Like my neighbors had a thirty-four-pound turkey. I didn't mind that so much. It's what they stuffed it with—a twenty-four-pound turkey.

I'm not going to go to my brother-in-law's anymore. Cheap? Last Thanksgiving he served a margarineball turkey!

An optimist is a turkey who spends the month before Thanksgiving going, "Moooo!"

Take my advice—never buy one of those frozen turkeys. We had one last year—eighteen pounds! When the goose bumps went down—two and a half!

I'll tell you how big this bird was. We stuffed it with bread crumb.

Thanksgiving is when the oven says to the turkey, "I'm hot for your body!"

I love those electric carving knives. Now you can be hurt worse than the turkey is!

The scene is the first Thanksgiving dinner. Two Indians finish their pumpkin pie, thank their hosts, and start walking back to their tribe. As they get out of earshot, one Indian says, "What did you think?" The other answers, "I'll tell you something—a Julia Child they're not!"

This morning my wife asked me what kind of cake she should make for Thanksgiving dinner. I said, "Are your relatives coming over?" She said, "Yes." I said, "How about sponge?"

Every year we have my wife's relatives over for a real old-fashioned Thanksgiving. We provide the giving and they provide the thanks.

I won't say how they ate but every two hours we stopped to carry out the wounded!

You have no idea how my wife's relatives can eat. One year I bent over to say grace and when I looked up again, somebody was handing me an after-dinner mint.

You should see the way they eat. You know how some people, after a meal, count the silver? We count the kids!

I really didn't have too much to eat at Thanksgiving dinner. My wife put the turkey on the table and said her uncle took care of the dressing. He's an expert on stuffing. I said, "Really? He's a chef?" She said, "No. A mortician."

My brother-in-law held up the wishbone and said, "Would you like to make a wish?" I said, "It's too late. You're here!"

I sat next to my brother-in-law. Course, I don't call him my brother-in-law. He's more like our resident tapeworm. . . . This man is to food what Anacin is to headaches!

Thanksgiving is a time that brings people together. I met a cousin I hadn't seen in twenty years. I said, "What have you been doing?" He said, "Twenty years!"

We had a wild Thanksgiving last year. I won the wishbone pull and my mother-in-law came down with food poisoning. I never knew those things worked!

One year I cooked the Thanksgiving dinner and my wife said, "That's what I call a surprise." Which was pretty nice of her. The doctor called it "ptomaine"!

My wife says it's a tom turkey but I'm not so sure. We can't get the wing off its hip!

We stuffed the turkey with oysters and it was very unusual. It's the first time I ever saw a turkey reading *Playboy*!

Kids are great at Thanksgiving. These three kids were talking and one of them said, "I'm gonna have three helpings of turkey, four helpings of stuffing, and five pieces of mince pie!" The second kid said, "I'm gonna have four helpings of turkey, five helpings of stuffing, and six pieces of mince pie!" The third kid said, "I'm gonna make a pig of myself!"

You know who I feel sorry for at Thanksgiving dinners? Weight Watchers! They must feel like the checkroom attendant at an orgy.

The problem with every Thanksgiving dinner is: The drinks go right to your head and the roast potatoes go right to your hips!

My wife is one of those creative cooks. You know how some people put stuffing in the turkey? She puts bicarbonate in. Why wait till the last minute?

And at the end of every Thanksgiving dinner we have a touch of the bubbly. A touch of the bubbly—Alka-Seltzer!

An optimist is anyone who has a twenty-eight-pound turkey for Thanksgiving—and the next day asks, "What's for lunch?"

The week after Thanksgiving is when you sit down to dinner and ask, "Are we having pheasant under glass?" And your wife answers, "No. We're having turkey under Saran wrap!"

It's the same thing every year. First you have roast turkey. Then the next day you have warmed-up turkey, followed by cold turkey, followed by turkey croquettes, followed by turkey omelette, followed by turkey hash, followed by turkey soup, followed by Christmas!

I never knew my wife saved leftovers until she gave me a turkey salad and there was something in it—tinsel.

I have a thing about leftovers. I won't even go out with a widow.

Show me a man who throws Thanksgiving leftovers into the garbage and I'll show you a fella who quits cold turkey!

THEFT

_____ has all kinds of legal gambling. If you want to take a chance in the morning, you can buy a lottery ticket. If you want to take a chance in the afternoon, you can bet on the horses. If you want to take a chance at night, you can play Bingo. And if you want to take a chance at midnight—you can walk to the corner.

You think I'm kidding? If you take a walk at two o'clock in the morning and you're not mugged—you start checking your deodorant.

Last year my neighbor was robbed of $60 so he went out and bought a hundred-pound police dog. In six months, the dog ate $752 worth of meat. Yesterday he got rid of the dog and asked the robber for a second chance!

When there's a will there's a way. We couldn't afford a watchdog so we did the next best thing. We taught the kids how to bark.

They even have a song about people who live in high-crime districts: "Button Up Your Overcoat, Someone Stole Your Pants."

It's such a friendly town. Last night alone we had three visitors. Two while we were home.

I didn't mind when they stole our black and white TV set. I didn't mind when they stole our color TV set. But when they changed the address on our subscription to *TV Guide*, that was going too far!

I stopped a burglary last night and it's only because I think fast on my feet. It's three o'clock in the morning and I see this fella tiptoeing into my living room. So, quick as a flash, I say to myself, "How many ballet dancers do I know?"

TRAVEL

The guy who said, "You can't take it with you," never saw my family pack for a trip.

I love to travel because it brings something into your life you never had before—poverty.

My favorite national park is Yellowstone—the only national park that's rated X. Somebody is always saying, "Don't look now, but there's a bear behind!"

The national parks are a very educational experience. The first thing you learn is never pat a bear on the head. And if you don't, the *last* thing you learn is never pat a bear on the head.

If you think it's a small world, try seeing it by bus.

Kids have a totally different way to pack for a three-month trip to Europe. They take one shirt, one pair of pants, one pair of sandals, and a change of guitar.

All you parents who have been saving for years and have never been able to get to Europe—it's easy. All you have to do is die and come back as a guitar!

It's so impressive being in St. Peter's Square. Where else can you see traffic signs that say KNEEL, DON'T KNEEL?

You have to give the Royal Family credit. When they hold their nose in the air, they look regal. When I do it, I fall downstairs.

TROUBLES

A loser is somebody who plays Monopoly and gets mugged on Boardwalk!

In this life, the quality of mercy is not strained—which explains why so many of us get our lumps!

Did you hear about the sex maniac who was pleading his own case and doing a great job—until he came to the summation. He said, "Ladies and gentlemen of the jury, I am innocent of this dastardly accusation and so I would like to throw myself on the mercy of the court—not to mention the blonde in the second row!"

You know you're a loser when certain things happen. Like yesterday a Good Humor man yelled at me.

We just don't look prosperous. I know we don't look prosperous. Every time the Avon lady comes she shows us seconds.

Nothing ever seems to go right for me. I have a canary who hums.

I was the only boy scout who couldn't start a fire by rubbing two sticks together. I either had to carry matches or Mrs. O'Leary's cow.

I'm so unlucky, if I bought an aspirin factory, they'd repeal the income tax.

I've always settled for second-best. Like I go to a dermatologist with acne.

You think you have troubles. My sundial is slow.

I'll tell you what kind of a life I've been leading. Last month my phone bill was $142—and this was just to Dial-A-Prayer!

I'm so nervous, what my cup runneth over is me!

I'm so insecure, I have a rowing machine with a life preserver!

You think you have troubles? I bought that washday miracle that makes my laundry smell as fresh as all outdoors—and I live in Bayonne! [LOCALIZE.]

I'm so discouraged, sometimes I wish Noah had built the *Titanic*.

I'll tell you what kind of a day I had. The car broke down going in to work. I had an argument with the boss. I lost my biggest account. The mechanic charged me $143 to fix the car. I got home, dropped into my favorite chair, and located the one egg we couldn't find at Easter.

You can't trust anything these days. I went into one of those little stores downtown, put a quarter into a machine marked PEEP SHOW, and got five minutes of the Hartz Mountain Canaries!

Did you ever have one of those days when everything goes wrong?

For instance, every year I've been going out to Chicago because I have relations there. My wife just found out with whom.

Do you ever get the feeling you're going nowhere—and have already arrived?

I dunno. Sometimes I feel like the nurse who gives Mickey Rooney his flu shots. I'm always getting the short end of things.

I knew I was in trouble when my mother-in-law showed up for a weekend visit with six suitcases and her cemetery deed.

Misery is having your wife clean your false teeth—
in the blender.

TURTLES

We have all kinds of pets. We have birds who specialize in singing; we have dogs who specialize in barking; we have cats who specialize in meowing; and we have turtles who specialize in dying.

Be honest now. Have you ever bought one of those turtles that lasted for more than a month? I can't understand it. I think they sell us geriatric turtles. . . . We have a fish bowl that's permanently in mourning.

I don't want to complain, but just once I'd like to get a turtle that isn't a factory second.

I figured it out: Last year I spent five hours planting seeds in my garden—and five weeks planting turtles.

Some fathers come home from work and ask, "What's new?" I ask, "Who went?"

I'll never forget what happened to our first turtle. I told my kid he should keep it in a bowl. He picked the one in the bathroom.

And it upset him because my kid is very conscious of money. You know how some kids have a pet turtle and on the shell it says SOUVENIR OF NEW YORK or SOUVENIR OF WASHINGTON, D.C.? He has one that says SOUVENIR OF 79¢ PLUS TAX!

The trouble with turtles is, you don't even know *when* they're dead.

They lie there for ten days, and just when you're getting ready to throw them out, they make a move. We have the same problem with our oldest son.

The big problem with turtles is feeding them. Turtles are just like kids. They never eat what you put in front of them. . . . You buy a dog, a hamster, or a canary and they eat everything. You buy a turtle and they're always on a diet!

And turtles spend a lot of time crawling all over each other—and so slowly. Looks like an orgy at Sun City.

Have you ever watched a turtle walk? They're so slow and careful and deliberate. You don't know whether to give them a push or the name of a good chiropodist!

UNEMPLOYMENT

Did you ever get the feeling prosperity *has* returned—but it can't get through the unemployment lines?

The two biggest problems facing America today: PARTISAN POLITICS: when you pass the buck. UNEMPLOYMENT: when the buck passes you!

The nice part about being unemployed is, when you turn over in the morning—you're there.

The problem with unemployment is: What do you do to pass the time? I know a fella who's in his sixth month of unemployment. His wife is in her sixth month too.

Unemployment is hitting youth the hardest. You can tell. Last week a collection agency repossessed six cars, nine TV sets, and three hundred guitars.

Four million kids are graduating this month and so far the only positions they've found are in sex manuals.

Incidentally, there's going to be a mass meeting of all the June college graduates who begin their new jobs next week. It'll be held in a Volkswagen.

Highly skilled people are so desperate for work, they'll take anything.

I was talking to a Ph.D. last week and I'll never forget what he said —"Fill 'er up?"

You have no idea how scarce jobs are these days. A personnel director asked a fella, "Do you lie, cheat, steal, or come in late?" He said, "No, but I can learn!"

Unemployment just hit a new high. If you don't believe it, yesterday an organ grinder's monkey died and he got forty-two applications— three from monkeys!

"The devil finds work for idle hands." Now if we could only get private industry to do the same!

UNIONS

Labor leaders are a peculiar mix of the old and the new—like a space capsule with a running board.

Talk about labor troubles: a Nevada house of ill repute had a strike and everything came to a grinding halt.

Now the gravediggers are out on strike. I tell you, it's enough to make a body pause.

I can't understand all these unions striking for shorter hours. What's wrong with sixty minutes?

I believe in the four-day week. It gives you more time to look for a second job.

A thought for unions making wage demands: Bankruptcy is also a closed shop.

UNITED NATIONS

The U.N. was created to give birth to peace. Peace is now in its 408th month.

Every time there's trouble like this, somebody calls the U.N. And the U.N. is finally doing something about it. It's getting an unlisted number.

A typical American is someone who feuds with his neighbors, argues with his employees, disagrees with minority groups, yells at his family—and can't understand why the United Nations don't get along with each other.

The U.N. is like a slot machine in Las Vegas. You keep feeding it money but it never pays off.

There is nothing like a vote at the U.N. to tell you who your friends were.

VACATIONS

I had a very unusual two-week vacation. I got on an elevator in an eighty-story building after a kid had pressed all the buttons!

We just got back into town, and you know that book that tells you how to have a wonderful vacation for ten dollars a day? Well, now I know how you do it. You stay home and read this book!

Believe me. If you ate at some of the places we did, ten dollars a day wouldn't cover the bicarbonate!

Let's face it. Vacations don't make sense. They really don't. You get in a car, drive 550 miles, and what do you spend all your time looking for? Home-cooked meals!

Don't you feel sorry for those people who go on vacation and spend all their time driving? My neighbor was telling me he drove 6,000 miles in two weeks. He said he even saw Washington, D.C. I said, "What was it like?" He said, "Three red lights and a green!"

I always take one of those "and up" vacations. You know the kind. Where the ad says "$299 and up." They call it "and up" because that's what you are all night trying to figure out how the total got to be $1,742!

There's one thing I can never understand about vacations. Every year we go away with three half-empty suitcases—and every year we come back with three bulging suitcases, two cardboard cartons, and four shopping bags, and I'm still the only tourist I know who carries dirty laundry in my wallet! . . . Which, after a three-week vacation, makes sense. It's the only place that's empty!

You can always tell how long a wife has been away from home by what her husband puts the dirty dishes in—the sink or the pool.

VALENTINE'S DAY

I always get kinda sentimental about Valentine's Day. I was telling my neighbor that every year I buy a card saying EVERYTHING I HAVE IS YOURS! He said, "Who do you send it to—your wife?" I said, "No. Internal Revenue!"

I don't mind telling you, I'm worried sick. I put a Valentine card and my income tax return into the same mail. Now I can't remember which one I signed GUESS WHO?

It's a funny thing about Valentine candy. By the time you get to the bottom of a five-pound box of chocolates, you can hardly lift yours.

And you can always tell a wife on February 14th. She's the only one who gets a Valentine card and says, "It's just what I wanted!"—while she's opening it up to look for the money!

My wife really is sentimental. One Valentine's Day I gave her a ring, and to this day, she has never forgotten those three little words that were engraved inside—MADE IN TAIWAN!

That's just like her. She loves to get in little digs. This morning she said she read the results of a survey that shows I'm sexier than average. I said, "Really? Where was the survey taken?" She said, "Forest Lawn."

Instead of giving your wife a mink coat, a diamond bracelet, or a sports car for Valentine's Day—give her a canary. Then, every time it opens its mouth, she'll think of you. Especially when it says, "CHEEP!"

That's right. If you're young and single—February 14th is a day of love and kisses and romance and tenderness. And if you've been married for twenty years—February 14th is the day after February 13th!

I know a fella who just sent out 40,000 Valentine cards doused in French perfume and signed "GUESS WHO?" He's a divorce lawyer.

You know what's fascinating? Valentine's Day at a mate-swapping club. On the top of each card it says: INITIAL AND PASS ON!

There's only one thing worse than your husband getting a passionate Valentine's Day card doused in perfume. That's his getting one doused in after-shave lotion!

VASECTOMY

A vasectomy is the stitch in time that saves nine.

They say a vasectomy doesn't affect your masculinity. So how come they give you *Playboy* on the way in and *Good Housekeeping* on the way out?

You know the worst thing that could happen with a vasectomy? You go into the hospital and the doctor who's going to do the operation is the fella your wife turned down to marry you. And he's standing there sterilizing the butter knife.

I'll tell you what *our* kids are like. Six teachers offered to chip in and buy me a vasectomy.

Show me a fella who becomes a father after having one of these operations—and I'll show you a half-vasectomy!

VOTING

I'll never forget the first time I voted in a presidential election. It was 1952 in Chicago. Come to think of it, I'll never forget the second, third, fourth, and fifth times I voted in a presidential election. It was 1952 in Chicago.

I'll vote for anybody who can figure out a way to take the preservatives out of our food and put them in our savings.

They say that 70 percent of major accidents originate in the home—and the rest in voting booths.

WALL STREET

I know an Indian whose name is Running Deer. He has a son on Wall Street. His name is Running Scared.

A Wall Street brokerage firm on the fortieth floor has a special sign for its customers: PLEASE DON'T STAND TOO NEAR AN OPEN WINDOW. YOUR TYPE OF PIGEON CAN'T FLY.

I happen to be a major holder on Wall Street—stock, bond, and bag.

Wall Street is where prophets tell us what will happen and profits tell us what did happen.

They say that women's clothes can predict the trend on Wall Street. If hemlines go up, the market goes up. If hemlines come down, the market goes down. Isn't that great? Yesterday I was a dirty old man. Today, a market analyst!

The problem with Wall Street is, it's a very sedentary business. If it wasn't for going like this [HIT YOUR FOREHEAD WITH THE PALM OF YOUR HAND], some investors wouldn't get any exercise at all!

It's just amazing how young financial analysts are these days. It's like I was saying to the head of a mutual fund as I helped him tie his shoelaces . . .

Personally, I have a diversified portfolio. That's when your money goes down the drain in six different sinks.

WASHINGTON (GEORGE)

George Washington is the one who sailed across the Delaware standing up. He must have had the same travel agent I do.

George Washington crossed the Delaware and caught the Hessians at Trenton. Or was it the Trentons at Heshing? Well, either way it was an embarrassing thing to be caught at!

George Washington was elected the first President of the United

States and for eight years nobody complained about the mess in Washington. Mostly because it was in Philadelphia.

"George Washington was first in war, first in peace, first in the hearts of his countrymen!" Which is all right if you like a pushy President.

They say George Washington had wooden teeth. Big deal. Our trumpet player has a tin ear.

George Washington had wooden teeth. He brushed after every meal and saw his carpenter twice a year.

Did you know that George Washington had wooden teeth? Wooden teeth! To George Washington, Polident was a nail!

Those were dramatic times in 1775. George Washington put in his wooden teeth; said, "I shall talk to the Army!"—and that's when things started clicking!

They say George Washington never told a lie. Then what's he doing on a dollar bill that's worth forty-three cents?

I don't want to brag, but I have a son who's a freshman and already he's following in George Washington's footsteps. He went down in history.

WATER POLLUTION

We can't procrastinate on pollution. Slime waits for no man!

Remember the good old days, when it was people who ran amuck—not faucets?

Isn't it wonderful how they're always thinking of new ways to protect us? Now there's a mouthwash for people who drink tap water.

Did you hear about the fella who jumped off the Brooklyn Bridge [LOCALIZE] and committed sewagecide?

Water pollution is so bad it's amazing. Yesterday we drove across the Hudson River [LOCALIZE]. What makes it so amazing, we didn't use the bridge!

Do you realize if George Washington were alive today, he could have *rolled* that dollar across a river?

It had to happen. The chemical formula for water is now H_2Ugh.

Water pollution has reached this stage: Last week a dam gave way and the lake didn't!

Water pollution is so bad, today it takes real courage to be a skin diver—or a Baptist.

Pollution today is so bad, walking on water is not only a miracle, but advisable!

Even the ocean is polluted. Last week I pulled a six-pound flounder out of the Atlantic. Today I got a thank-you note from his parents.

We've got to do something about water pollution. My kid has a water pistol that jams!

I'm really worried. He could be the first ten-year-old ever arrested for carrying a congealed weapon!

The water in this town is incredible. I'm beginning to think City Hall asked Mexico for the recipe!

Water is so polluted, now I know why herring get pickled!

I'll tell you how bad water pollution is. Yesterday I heard a voice saying, "All ashore that's going ashore." It was a fish!

You want to know what the water in Lake Erie is like? Wait, I'll get you a slice.

Let me put it this way: This is the only state where the water needs tenderizer.

A little song dedicated to pollution: "We Were Walking Along on Moonlight Bay."

I just saw an interesting sign. It said: DON'T THROW ROCKS IN THE RIVER. IT DENTS THE WATER.

WAX FRUIT

My mother always did things in a big way. You know how some mothers had wax apples, pears, and grapes on the dining room table? She had a wax watermelon.

When I was a kid, every dining room table had a bowl of wax fruit on it. We had so much wax fruit in our neighborhood, if a house caught fire it burned for three months!

And it was a point of pride to have the most realistic wax fruit in the neighborhood. We had wax fruit that looked so real, we used to get nasty letters from ants!

Our wax fruit looked so real, we never knew Uncle Louie was near-sighted until we found something in the wax apple—Uncle Louie!

WEATHER

The Weather Bureau isn't taking any chances. It just predicted SLIGHTLY CLOUDY—WITH DRIFTS UP TO THREE FEET.

Lincoln was wrong. There is one man who can fool all of the people all the time—and I'd like to introduce him to you. Our weatherman!

We have a wonderful weatherman. Last week he predicted a 30 percent chance of rain. I heard it just before the radio floated out the window.

Isn't this rain something? You get home, take off your clothes, and it's one damp thing after another!

People keep asking me how I made out during the floods.
Come over and see. It's the house with the periscope.

I have to be honest. I didn't even know it was a flood. We've been trying to housebreak a Great Dane.

This is the time of year when the seasons overlap. When you put on snow tires to go to the beach.

WEDDINGS

Have you noticed how everything in a wedding is set up for the bride? She carries a beautiful bouquet of flowers; she wears a $600 gown, and the organ plays "Here Comes the Bride." Where's the groom? He's out in the hall wearing a Hertz Rent-A-Tux. . . . I say Hertz 'cause the pants are too tight. . . . He doesn't know where the tux came from but every time they play slow music, the arms cross. . . .

And thanks to women's lib, we're really having some exciting weddings. One preacher said to the bride, "Do you promise to obey?" She said, "Do you think I'm crazy?" And the groom said, "I do!"

And you know the most ridiculous thing you can tell a mother at a wedding? "You're not losing a daughter. You're gaining a son!" At her age, that's all she needs. More children!

A Fire Island wedding ceremony is where they say to the mother of the groom, "Sarah, look at it this way: You're not losing a son. You're gaining a son!"

Two women were talking at a $10,000 catered wedding. One said, "She's just marrying him for a cheap thrill." The father of the bride tapped her on the shoulder. He said, "Thrill, maybe. Cheap, never!"

You know what a caterer is. That's a vacuum cleaner for money.

I get a little sad when I look at a wedding cake. It always reminds me of middle age—fat on the bottom and thin on top.

WEIGHT WATCHERS

Did you ever stop to think that Weight Watchers and women's liberation have the same objective—to cut men down to size?

Is it true Weight Watchers have a new motto: TUBBY OR NOT TUBBY, THAT IS THE QUESTION?

Show me a mother who joins Weight Watchers and I'll show you a maximum!

The best place to join a Weight Watchers club is Las Vegas. Do you know what they do in Las Vegas to cheaters?

Is it true that Weight Watchers is making a special appeal to office workers? And anybody else whose problem is stuffed drawers?

Have you ever gone to a Weight Watchers meeting? It's fantastic. Every week these people lose enough weight to build six Mickey Rooneys!

Did you hear about the group of Weight Watchers that expelled one of its members? The one who burped?

I had a weird dream. I was at this big dinner and we had chopped chicken liver, lobster bisque, sirloin steak smothered in fried onions, a baked potato stuffed with sour cream, broccoli dripping with Hollandaise sauce, hot buttered rolls, and pecan pie topped with whipped cream. Then the master of ceremonies stood up and said, "Fellow Weight Watchers . . ."

King Kong is 90 feet tall and weighs 28,000 pounds. In the new version he's chased by the cops, the Army, the Air Force, and Weight Watchers!

WHITE HOUSE

On-the-job training is a device used for office boys, laborers, and Presidents of the United States.

The President had a traumatic thing happen to him this week. He was taking a walk outside the White House when a tourist couple ran up to him with a camera and said, "Mr. President, we know this is a terrible imposition, but would you mind?" The President said, "Of course not." So they gave him the camera and posed in front of their car.

Someone said the President is ignoring the will of the American people. I didn't even know we had died.

We may have been better off when Presidents tried to make history rather than the eleven o'clock news.

I think it's wonderful the way the White House is economizing. It's the first time I ever drank a '69 vintage and it was Kool-Aid.

WIVES

My wife is sixteen years old. I think the only reason she married me was to get into R-rated movies.

My wife is half-Irish, half-Italian. When I married her the only thing she made was potatoes—and she mashed them with her feet!

My wife keeps saying, "I want a man who'll look up to me." So I introduced her to a jockey.

My wife is very hostile. This morning she called me sugar, sweetie, and honey. That doesn't sound hostile? A lot you know—I'm a diabetic!

Yesterday she said, "I should have seen through you when you took me into that store to pick a wedding ring." I said, "What's wrong with that?" She said, "It was a hardware store!"

My wife is always putting me out of the bedroom. I've spent so much time sleeping on the couch, I have an ingrown cushion.

My wife keeps saying, "I've given you the best years of my life!" I don't know if she wants a divorce or a receipt.

One time I accused my wife of having no sense of humor. She said, "You've got to be kidding. I even have an official document that says I have a sense of humor." I said, "What document?" She said, "Our marriage license."

My wife gets mad because I never shave on weekends. She says if I'm away and she gets lonesome, she kisses a Brillo pad.

My wife has a truck rental attitude toward garbage. Whenever it has to be taken out, she says, "U-Haul!"

After every Saturday night party, I always send flowers to my wife. If I don't know why, she does!

Let's be practical about this. The only time you should ever put a wife on a pedestal is when the ceiling needs painting.

If you really want to make your wife feel good, the next time she comes out of the shower, say, "I like that outfit. I saw one just like it in *Playboy*."

I found out how my wife feels about food on our very first date. I took her home and she slipped into something cool—the refrigerator!

WIGS

My wife is always looking for bargains. She has the only wig in town with split ends.

My wife has a wig that's made in Germany. So far three combs have confessed!

Talk about shrewd. I know a fella who gave his wife six different wigs. No matter what color hair she finds on his collar, he's covered!

Men, take my advice. Don't ever buy a cheap toupee. Now I'm losing hair that isn't even mine!

WINTER

Nothing hits me in the gizzard,
Like waking up to see a blizzard.
I hear the radiator clank and hiss,
Then turn on the air conditioner to reminisce.
The wind cuts deep with every raw gust;
How come we prayed for this in August?

I love to get up on these cold winter mornings—when there's a real nip in the smog!

Isn't this weather invigorating? I was telling my neighbor, "Every morning I get up and jig for twenty minutes." He said, "You mean jog." I said, "Jig. The door sticks on our bathroom!"

Yesterday the temperature went down to zero. First time I ever saw anybody mugged for their mittens!

You know, I could never understand why they make kids wear mittens. Like, that's all a five-year-old needs—something to make him more clumsy!

Having spent a good part of the last six months pushing a lawn mower, I look forward to winter. Winter is nature's way of freezing your grass off.

I know a long-suffering husband who has just one complaint about November. Not only is the frost on the pumpkin but he thinks a little of it got on his wife.

Our storm windows have really kept my wife warm this winter. I didn't put them up and is she hot about it.

X-rated movies are ideal for cold weather. At least you have a reason for coming out with your collar turned up.

I don't mind telling you, I had one of the most marvelous Januarys ever. I took up smoking, drinking, gambling, and running around with women—just so I'd have something to give up for Lent!

January is when you buy the forty-five dollars' worth of Christmas cards at half price—you won't be able to locate next December.

WOMEN'S LIBERATION

Women are indeed an admirable sex. Through the centuries they've been wept upon, stepped upon, crept upon, and slept upon—and yet they still find something in men to love!

Did you ever get the feeling that women's liberation has gone too far? I mean, I just heard the Boston Moms Orchestra.

Then there's the women's liberation breakfast cereal. It goes snap, crackle, and mom!

"I know a fella who gets very upset when he's called a male chauvinist pig."
"He's a liberal?"
"He's a rabbi."

I went to a Women's Liberation Wild Boar Barbecue and was having a wonderful time until I realized what I was eating—a male chauvinist pig.

Women's liberation has done wonders for the guilt feelings of American men. Yesterday I had a seat on a crowded bus and a woman was standing in front of me. I said, "Pardon me, but are you a member of women's liberation?" She said, "Yes, I am." I said, "Is that the organization that wants women to stand on their own two feet?" She said, "Yes, it is." I said, "Right on!"

Psychological warfare is a husband saying, "You want equal rights? Okay—*you* kill the mouse!"

Thanks to women's liberation, women are now the absolute equals of men. Men have always believed in free love. Now women believe in free love. Men have always raised hell on Saturday night. Now women raise hell on Saturday night. Men have always picked up the check. Now women raise hell on Saturday night.

There's a lot of talk about women's liberation, but when all is said and done, men still have the last word. It's "Yes, dear."

Women are confused as to which sexual identity to assume. I know my wife is. She still nags but in a much deeper voice.

I'll believe in women's liberation when it spends $2 million to build a home for unwed fathers.

WORLD CONDITIONS

The Middle East deadlock is like a bagel. The longer it lasts, the harder it is to break.

The nice part about having rotten kids is, you don't feel so guilty about the world you're giving them.

If the meek ever do inherit this earth, my advice to them is get a good lawyer and fight the case!

Fascism is never having to say you're sorry.

X-RATED MOVIES

It shows you how times have changed. In 1848 Karl Marx wrote: "Workers of the world, unite!" And it was called communism. Now it's called X-rated movies.

X pictures are the ones you have to worry about. You're never sure if X is the rating or the signature of the people who made them!

The Germans have a way with words. They don't call them X-rated movies—Puffinpantinflickenlooken!

You can't win. I wanted to see an X-rated movie and the cashier wouldn't sell me a ticket. Said she had a headache.

I saw my first X-rated movie last night and I was so shocked, I could hardly sit through it the third time.

I'm involved in a rather interesting experiment. I'm trying to convince my wife the movies I go to are not rated X. It's a V with an arch support.

Isn't that sweet? An X-rated movie house went out of business and they held a bon voyeur party.

Anyone who can yawn at an X-rated movie is suffering from indecent composure.

My neighbor is suffering from a skin problem. Spent six hours in an X-rated movie.

Don't you feel a little foolish, necking in a drive-in movie, when up on the screen they're doing it so much better?

I saw another movie they called a "family picture." I don't know who the family is but I think it's De Sade!

And the service in these theaters is fantastic. An usher leads you in and a cop leads you out!

Those adult movies are becoming more realistic. They just made one for couples who have been married twenty-five years. The fella walks into this room stark naked and the girl has a headache.

My wife and I went to see an X-rated movie at a drive-in theater and it was fascinating. I came back from the washroom and I said, "What did I miss?" She said [POINTING TO EITHER SIDE], "Two of that and one of that!"

I was watching one of these movies and the fella sitting next to me said, "In thirty years I haven't seen anything like this!" I said, "You've been a movie fan for thirty years?" He said, "No. A gynecologist!"

MELVIN POWERS SELF-IMPROVEMENT LIBRARY

ASTROLOGY

____ASTROLOGY—HOW TO CHART YOUR HOROSCOPE Max Heindel 7.00
____ASTROLOGY AND SEXUAL ANALYSIS Morris C. Goodman 10.00
____ASTROLOGY AND YOU Carroll Righter 5.00
____ASTROLOGY MADE EASY Astarte 7.00
____ASTROLOGY, ROMANCE, YOU AND THE STARS Anthony Norvell 10.00
____MY WORLD OF ASTROLOGY Sydney Omarr 10.00
____THOUGHT DIAL Sydney Omarr 7.00
____WHAT THE STARS REVEAL ABOUT THE MEN IN YOUR LIFE Thelma White 3.00

BRIDGE

____BRIDGE BIDDING MADE EASY Edwin B. Kantar 15.00
____BRIDGE CONVENTIONS Edwin B. Kantar 10.00
____COMPETITIVE BIDDING IN MODERN BRIDGE Edgar Kaplan 7.00
____DEFENSIVE BRIDGE PLAY COMPLETE Edwin B Kantar 20.00
____GAMESMAN BRIDGE—PLAY BETTER WITH KANTAR Edwin B. Kantar 7.00
____HOW TO IMPROVE YOUR BRIDGE Alfred Sheinwold 7.00
____IMPROVING YOUR BIDDING SKILLS Edwin B. Kantar 10.00
____INTRODUCTION TO DECLARER'S PLAY Edwin B. Kantar 10.00
____INTRODUCTION TO DEFENDER'S PLAY Edwin B. Kantar 10.00
____KANTAR FOR THE DEFENSE Edwin B. Kantar 10.00
____KANTAR FOR THE DEFENSE VOLUME 2 Edwin B. Kantar 10.00
____TEST YOUR BRIDGE PLAY Edwin B. Kantar 10.00
____VOLUME 2—TEST YOUR BRIDGE PLAY Edwin B. Kantar 10.00
____WINNING DECLARER PLAY Dorothy Hayden Truscott 10.00

BUSINESS, STUDY & REFERENCE

____BRAINSTORMING Charles Clark 10.00
____CONVERSATION MADE EASY Elliot Russell 5.00
____EXAM SECRET Dennis B. Jackson 7.00
____FIX-IT BOOK Arthur Symons 2.00
____HOW TO DEVELOP A BETTER SPEAKING VOICE M. Hellier 5.00
____HOW TO SAVE 50% ON GAS & CAR EXPENSES Ken Stansbie 5.00
____HOW TO SELF-PUBLISH YOUR BOOK & MAKE IT A BEST SELLER Melvin Powers . . 20.00
____INCREASE YOUR LEARNING POWER Geoffrey A. Dudley 5.00
____PRACTICAL GUIDE TO BETTER CONCENTRATION Melvin Powers 5.00
____PUBLIC SPEAKING MADE EASY Thomas Montalbo 10.00
____7 DAYS TO FASTER READING William S. Schaill 7.00
____SONGWRITER'S RHYMING DICTIONARY Jane Shaw Whitfield 10.00
____SPELLING MADE EASY Lester D. Basch & Dr. Milton Finkelstein 3.00
____STUDENT'S GUIDE TO BETTER GRADES J.A. Rickard 3.00
____YOUR WILL & WHAT TO DO ABOUT IT Attorney Samuel G. King 7.00

CALLIGRAPHY

____ADVANCED CALLIGRAPHY Katherine Jeffares 7.00
____CALLIGRAPHY—THE ART OF BEAUTIFUL WRITING Katherine Jeffares 7.00
____CALLIGRAPHY FOR FUN & PROFIT Anne Leptich & Jacque Evans 10.00
____CALLIGRAPHY MADE EASY Tina Serafini 7.00

CHESS & CHECKERS

____BEGINNER'S GUIDE TO WINNING CHESS Fred Reinfeld 10.00
____CHESS IN TEN EASY LESSONS Larry Evans 10.00
____CHESS MADE EASY Milton L. Hanauer 5.00
____CHESS PROBLEMS FOR BEGINNERS Edited by Fred Reinfeld 7.00
____CHESS TACTICS FOR BEGINNERS Edited by Fred Reinfeld 10.00

_____HOW TO WIN AT CHECKERS Fred Reinfeld 7.00
_____1001 BRILLIANT WAYS TO CHECKMATE Fred Reinfeld 10.00
_____1001 WINNING CHESS SACRIFICES & COMBINATIONS Fred Reinfeld 10.00

COOKERY & HERBS

_____CULPEPER'S HERBAL REMEDIES Dr. Nicholas Culpeper 5.00
_____FAST GOURMET COOKBOOK Poppy Cannon 2.50
_____HEALING POWER OF HERBS May Bethel 5.00
_____HEALING POWER OF NATURAL FOODS May Bethel 7.00
_____HERBS FOR HEALTH—HOW TO GROW & USE THEM Louise Evans Doole 7.00
_____HOME GARDEN COOKBOOK—DELICIOUS NATURAL FOOD RECIPES Ken Kraft 3.00
_____MEATLESS MEAL GUIDE Tomi Ryan & James H. Ryan, M.D. 4.00
_____VEGETABLE GARDENING FOR BEGINNERS Hugh Wilberg 2.00
_____VEGETABLES FOR TODAY'S GARDENS R. Milton Carleton 2.00
_____VEGETARIAN COOKERY Janet Walker 10.00
_____VEGETARIAN COOKING MADE EASY & DELECTABLE Veronica Vezza 3.00

GAMBLING & POKER

_____HOW TO WIN AT POKER Terence Reese & Anthony T. Watkins 10.00
_____SCARNE ON DICE John Scarne 15.00
_____WINNING AT CRAPS Dr. Lloyd T. Commins 10.00
_____WINNING AT GIN Chester Wander & Cy Rice 10.00
_____WINNING AT POKER—AN EXPERT'S GUIDE John Archer 10.00
_____WINNING AT 21—AN EXPERT'S GUIDE John Archer 10.00
_____WINNING POKER SYSTEMS Norman Zadeh 10.00

HEALTH

_____BEE POLLEN Lynda Lyngheim & Jack Scagnetti 5.00
_____COPING WITH ALZHEIMER'S Rose Oliver, Ph.D. & Francis Bock, Ph.D. 10.00
_____DR. LINDNER'S POINT SYSTEM FOOD PROGRAM Peter G Lindner, M.D. 2.00
_____HELP YOURSELF TO BETTER SIGHT Margaret Darst Corbett 10.00
_____HOW YOU CAN STOP SMOKING PERMANENTLY Ernest Caldwell 5.00
_____NATURE'S WAY TO NUTRITION & VIBRANT HEALTH Robert J. Scrutton 3.00
_____NEW CARBOHYDRATE DIET COUNTER Patti Lopez-Pereira 2.00
_____REFLEXOLOGY Dr. Maybelle Segal 7.00
_____REFLEXOLOGY FOR GOOD HEALTH Anna Kaye & Don C. Matchan 10.00
_____30 DAYS TO BEAUTIFUL LEGS Dr. Marc Selner 3.00
_____YOU CAN LEARN TO RELAX Dr. Samuel Gutwirth 5.00

HOBBIES

_____BEACHCOMBING FOR BEGINNERS Norman Hickin 2.00
_____BLACKSTONE'S MODERN CARD TRICKS Harry Blackstone 10.00
_____BLACKSTONE'S SECRETS OF MAGIC Harry Blackstone 7.00
_____COIN COLLECTING FOR BEGINNERS Burton Hobson & Fred Reinfeld 7.00
_____ENTERTAINING WITH ESP Tony 'Doc' Shiels 2.00
_____400 FASCINATING MAGIC TRICKS YOU CAN DO Howard Thurston 7.00
_____HOW I TURN JUNK INTO FUN AND PROFIT Sari 3.00
_____HOW TO WRITE A HIT SONG AND SELL IT Tommy Boyce 10.00
_____MAGIC FOR ALL AGES Walter Gibson 10.00
_____PLANTING A TREE TreePeople with Andy & Katie Lipkis 13.00
_____STAMP COLLECTING FOR BEGINNERS Burton Hobson 3.00

HORSE PLAYERS' WINNING GUIDES

_____BETTING HORSES TO WIN Les Conklin 10.00
_____ELIMINATE THE LOSERS Bob McKnight 5.00
_____HOW TO PICK WINNING HORSES Bob McKnight 5.00
_____HOW TO WIN AT THE RACES Sam (The Genius) Lewin 5.00
_____HOW YOU CAN BEAT THE RACES Jack Kavanagh 5.00
_____MAKING MONEY AT THE RACES David Barr 7.00

___PAYDAY AT THE RACES Les Conklin 7.00
___SMART HANDICAPPING MADE EASY William Bauman 5.00
___SUCCESS AT THE HARNESS RACES Barry Meadow 7.00

HUMOR
___HOW TO FLATTEN YOUR TUSH Coach Marge Reardon 2.00
___JOKE TELLER'S HANDBOOK Bob Orben 10.00
___JOKES FOR ALL OCCASIONS Al Schock 7.00
___2,000 NEW LAUGHS FOR SPEAKERS Bob Orben 7.00
___2,400 JOKES TO BRIGHTEN YOUR SPEECHES Robert Orben 10.00
___2,500 JOKES TO START'EM LAUGHING Bob Orben 10.00

HYPNOTISM
___CHILDBIRTH WITH HYPNOSIS William S. Kroger, M.D. 5.00
___HOW YOU CAN BOWL BETTER USING SELF-HYPNOSIS Jack Heise 7.00
___HOW YOU CAN PLAY BETTER GOLF USING SELF-HYPNOSIS Jack Heise 3.00
___HYPNOSIS AND SELF-HYPNOSIS Bernard Hollander, M.D. 7.00
___HYPNOTISM (Originally published 1893) Carl Sextus 5.00
___HYPNOTISM MADE EASY Dr. Ralph Winn................................. 10.00
___HYPNOTISM MADE PRACTICAL Louis Orton 5.00
___MODERN HYPNOSIS Lesley Kuhn & Salvatore Russo, Ph.D. 5.00
___NEW CONCEPTS OF HYPNOSIS Bernard C. Gindes, M.D. 10.00
___NEW SELF-HYPNOSIS Paul Adams 10.00
___POST-HYPNOTIC INSTRUCTIONS—SUGGESTIONS FOR THERAPY Arnold Furst ... 10.00
___PRACTICAL GUIDE TO SELF-HYPNOSIS Melvin Powers 10.00
___PRACTICAL HYPNOTISM Philip Magonet, M.D. 3.00
___SECRETS OF HYPNOTISM S.J. Van Pelt, M.D. 5.00
___SELF-HYPNOSIS—A CONDITIONED-RESPONSE TECHNIQUE Laurence Sparks 7.00
___SELF-HYPNOSIS—ITS THEORY, TECHNIQUE & APPLICATION Melvin Powers 7.00
___THERAPY THROUGH HYPNOSIS Edited by Raphael H. Rhodes 5.00

JUDAICA
___SERVICE OF THE HEART Evelyn Garfiel, Ph.D. 10.00
___STORY OF ISRAEL IN COINS Jean & Maurice Gould 2.00
___STORY OF ISRAEL IN STAMPS Maxim & Gabriel Shamir 1.00
___TONGUE OF THE PROPHETS Robert St. John 10.00

JUST FOR WOMEN
___COSMOPOLITAN'S GUIDE TO MARVELOUS MEN Foreword by Helen Gurley Brown .. 3.00
___COSMOPOLITAN'S HANG-UP HANDBOOK Foreword by Helen Gurley Brown 4.00
___COSMOPOLITAN'S LOVE BOOK—A GUIDE TO ECSTASY IN BED 7.00
___COSMOPOLITAN'S NEW ETIQUETTE GUIDE Foreword by Helen Gurley Brown 4.00
___I AM A COMPLEAT WOMAN Doris Hagopian & Karen O'Connor Sweeney 3.00
___JUST FOR WOMEN—A GUIDE TO THE FEMALE BODY Richard E. Sand M.D. 5.00
___NEW APPROACHES TO SEX IN MARRIAGE John E. Eichenlaub, M.D. 3.00
___SEXUALLY ADEQUATE FEMALE Frank S. Caprio, M.D. 3.00
___SEXUALLY FULFILLED WOMAN Dr. Rachel Copelan 5.00

MARRIAGE, SEX & PARENTHOOD
___ABILITY TO LOVE Dr. Allan Fromme 7.00
___GUIDE TO SUCCESSFUL MARRIAGE Drs. Albert Ellis & Robert Harper 10.00
___HOW TO RAISE AN EMOTIONALLY HEALTHY, HAPPY CHILD Albert Ellis, Ph.D. 10.00
___PARENT SURVIVAL TRAINING Marvin Silverman, Ed.D. & David Lustig, Ph.D. 15.00
___POTENCY MIRACLE Uri P. Peles, M.D. 10.00
___SEX WITHOUT GUILT Albert Ellis, Ph.D. 7.00
___SEXUALLY ADEQUATE MALE Frank S. Caprio, M.D. 3.00
___SEXUALLY FULFILLED MAN Dr. Rachel Copelan 5.00
___STAYING IN LOVE Dr. Norton F. Kristy 7.00

MELVIN POWERS MAIL ORDER LIBRARY

____ HOW TO GET RICH IN MAIL ORDER Melvin Powers 20.00
____ HOW TO SELF-PUBLISH YOUR BOOK Melvin Powers 20.00
____ HOW TO WRITE A GOOD ADVERTISEMENT Victor O. Schwab 20.00
____ MAIL ORDER MADE EASY J. Frank Brumbaugh 20.00
____ MAKING MONEY WITH CLASSIFIED ADS Melvin Powers 20.00

METAPHYSICS & NEW AGE

____ CONCENTRATION—A GUIDE TO MENTAL MASTERY Mouni Sadhu 10.00
____ EXTRA-TERRESTRIAL INTELLIGENCE—THE FIRST ENCOUNTER 6.00
____ FORTUNE TELLING WITH CARDS P. Foli 10.00
____ HOW TO INTERPRET DREAMS, OMENS & FORTUNE TELLING SIGNS Gettings 5.00
____ HOW TO UNDERSTAND YOUR DREAMS Geoffrey A. Dudley 7.00
____ MAGICIAN—HIS TRAINING AND WORK W.E. Butler 7.00
____ MEDITATION Mouni Sadhu 10.00
____ NUMEROLOGY—ITS FACTS AND SECRETS Ariel Yvon Taylor 5.00
____ NUMEROLOGY MADE EASY W. Mykian 5.00
____ PALMISTRY MADE EASY Fred Gettings 7.00
____ PALMISTRY MADE PRACTICAL Elizabeth Daniels Squire 7.00
____ PROPHECY IN OUR TIME Martin Ebon 2.50
____ SUPERSTITION—ARE YOU SUPERSTITIOUS? Eric Maple 2.00
____ TAROT OF THE BOHEMIANS Papus 10.00
____ WAYS TO SELF-REALIZATION Mouni Sadhu 7.00
____ WITCHCRAFT, MAGIC & OCCULTISM—A FASCINATING HISTORY W.B. Crow 10.00
____ WITCHCRAFT—THE SIXTH SENSE Justine Glass 7.00

RECOVERY

____ KNIGHT IN RUSTY ARMOR Robert Fisher 5.00
____ KNIGHTS WITHOUT ARMOR (Hardcover edition) Aaron R. Kipnis, Ph.D. 10.00
____ PRINCESS WHO BELIEVED IN FAIRY TALES Marcia Grad 10.00

SELF-HELP & INSPIRATIONAL

____ CHANGE YOUR VOICE, CHANGE YOUR LIFE Morton Cooper, Ph.D. 10.00
____ CHARISMA—HOW TO GET "THAT SPECIAL MAGIC" Marcia Grad 10.00
____ DAILY POWER FOR JOYFUL LIVING Dr. Donald Curtis 7.00
____ DYNAMIC THINKING Melvin Powers 5.00
____ GREATEST POWER IN THE UNIVERSE U.S. Andersen 10.00
____ GROW RICH WHILE YOU SLEEP Ben Sweetland 10.00
____ GROW RICH WITH YOUR MILLION DOLLAR MIND Brian Adams 7.00
____ GROWTH THROUGH REASON Albert Ellis, Ph.D. 10.00
____ GUIDE TO PERSONAL HAPPINESS Albert Ellis, Ph.D. & Irving Becker, Ed.D. 10.00
____ GUIDE TO RATIONAL LIVING Albert Ellis, Ph.D. & R. Harper, Ph.D. 15.00
____ HANDWRITING ANALYSIS MADE EASY John Marley 10.00
____ HANDWRITING TELLS Nadya Olyanova 10.00
____ HOW TO ATTRACT GOOD LUCK A.H.Z. Carr 10.00
____ HOW TO DEVELOP A WINNING PERSONALITY Martin Panzer 10.00
____ HOW TO DEVELOP AN EXCEPTIONAL MEMORY Young & Gibson 10.00
____ HOW TO LIVE WITH A NEUROTIC Albert Ellis, Ph.D. 10.00
____ HOW TO MAKE $100,000 A YEAR IN SALES Albert Winnikoff 15.00
____ HOW TO OVERCOME YOUR FEARS M.P. Leahy, M.D. 3.00
____ HOW TO SUCCEED Brian Adams 10.00
____ HUMAN PROBLEMS & HOW TO SOLVE THEM Dr. Donald Curtis 5.00
____ I CAN Ben Sweetland 10.00
____ I WILL Ben Sweetland 10.00
____ KNIGHT IN RUSTY ARMOR Robert Fisher 5.00
____ MAGIC IN YOUR MIND U.S. Andersen 15.00
____ MAGIC OF THINKING SUCCESS Dr. David J. Schwartz 10.00
____ MAGIC POWER OF YOUR MIND Walter M. Germain 10.00
____ NEVER UNDERESTIMATE THE SELLING POWER OF A WOMAN Dottie Walters 7.00

Available from your bookstore or directly from Melvin Powers.
Please add $2.00 shipping and handling for each book ordered.

Melvin Powers

12015 Sherman Road, No. Hollywood, California 91605

For our complete catalog, visit our Web site at http://www.mpowers.com.

Books by Melvin Powers

HOW TO GET RICH IN MAIL ORDER

1. How to Develop Your Mail Order Expertise 2. How to Find a Unique Product or Service to Sell 3. How to Make Money with Classified Ads 4. How to Make Money with Display Ads 5. The Unlimited Potential for Making Money with Direct Mail 6. How to Copycat Successful Mail Order Operations 7. How I Created a Bestseller Using the Copycat Technique 8. How to Start and Run a Profitable Mail Order Special Interest Book Business 9. I Enjoy Selling Books by Mail—Some of My Successful Ads 10. Five of My Most Successful Direct Mail Pieces That Sold and Are Selling Millions of Dollars' Worth of Books 11. Melvin Powers's Mail Order Success Strategy—Follow it and You'll Become a Millionaire 12. How to Sell Your Products to Mail Order Companies, Retail Outlets, Jobbers, and Fund Raisers for Maximum Distribution and Profit 13. How to Get Free Display Ads and Publicity that Will Put You on the Road to Riches 14. How to Make Your Advertising Copy Sizzle 15. Questions and Answers to Help You Get Started Making Money 16. A Personal Word from Melvin Powers 17. How to Get Started 18. Selling Products on Television   8½" x 11½" — 352 Pages . . . $20.00

MAKING MONEY WITH CLASSIFIED ADS

1. Getting Started with Classified Ads 2. Everyone Loves to Read Classified Ads 3. How to Find a Money-Making Product 4. How to Write Classified Ads that Make Money 5. What I've Learned from Running Thousands of Classified Ads 6. Classified Ads Can Help You Make Big Money in Multi-Level Programs 7. Two-Step Classified Ads Made Me a Multi-Millionaire—They Can Do the Same for You! 8. One-Inch Display Ads Can Work Wonders 9. Display Ads Can Make You a Fortune Overnight 10. Although I Live in California, I Buy My Grapefruit from Florida 11. Nuts and Bolts of Mail Order Success 12. What if You Can't Get Your Business Running Successfully? What's Wrong? How to Correct it 13. Strategy for Mail Order Success   8½" x 11½" — 240 Pages . . . $20.00

HOW TO SELF-PUBLISH YOUR BOOK AND HAVE THE FUN AND EXCITEMENT OF BEING A BEST-SELLING AUTHOR

1. Who is Melvin Powers? 2. What is the Motivation Behind Your Decision to Publish Your Book? 3. Why You Should Read This Chapter Even if You Already Have an Idea for a Book 4. How to Test the Salability of Your Book Before You Write One Word 5. How I Achieved Sales Totaling $2,000,000 on My Book *How to Get Rich in Mail Order* 6. How to Develop a Second Career by Using Your Expertise 7. How to Choose an Enticing Book Title 8. Marketing Strategy 9. Success Stories 10. How to Copyright Your Book 11. How to Write a Winning Advertisement 12. Advertising that Money Can't Buy 13. Questions and Answers to Help You Get Started 14. Self-Publishing and the Midas Touch
8½" x 11½" — 240 Pages . . . $20.00

A PRACTICAL GUIDE TO SELF-HYPNOSIS

1. What You Should Know about Self-Hypnosis 2. What about the Dangers of Hypnosis? 3. Is Hypnosis the Answer? 4. How Does Self-Hypnosis Work? 5. How to Arouse Yourself From the Self-Hypnotic State 6. How to Attain Self-Hypnosis 7. Deepening the Self-Hypnotic State 8. What You Should Know about Becoming an Excellent Subject 9. Techniques for Reaching the Somnambulistic State 10. A New Approach to Self-Hypnosis 11. Psychological Aids and Their Function 12. Practical Applications of Self-Hypnosis
144 Pages . . . $10.00

Available at your bookstore or directly from Melvin Powers.
Please add $2.00 shipping and handling for each book ordered.

Melvin Powers
12015 Sherman Road, No. Hollywood, California 91605

For our complete catalog, visit our Web site at http://www.mpowers.com.